Praise for *The Potential Principle*

"Potential was always a negative term. It meant what you could be but aren't. Mark has created a blueprint to turn your potential into reality. Everyone who thinks they have more in them should read this book."

—Scott Stratten, president of UnMarketing
Inc., bestselling author

"*The Potential Principle* not only reminds you that you can always get better, it gives you the precise blueprint for doing just that. A must read for high achievers!"

—Jay Baer, president of Convince &
Convert and author of *Hug Your Haters*

"Our company founder had a belief that we should 're-earn our positions every day in every way.' Mark has revealed the treasure map to get there—I am reenergized."

—Dina Dwyer-Owens, cochairman of the
Dwyer Group and author of *Values, Inc.*

"If you've ever wondered, *Can I do better?* this book is for you. If you've ever dreamed of going beyond your best, don't miss Mark Sanborn's *The Potential Principle*."

—Jeff Goins, bestselling author of *The Art
of Work* and *Real Artists Don't Starve*

"Mark Sanborn's sage advice to disrupt yourself is spot on. *The Potential Principle* will turbocharge your next level of success. The future belongs to those who keep getting better."

—Robert B. Tucker, author of
Innovation Is Everybody's Business

"*The Potential Principle* is absolutely amazing. After being successful in several areas of my life I got a wake-up call from Mark Sanborn. Reading this and realizing 'how good I can be' shifted me into another gear. Master the Potential Matrix and witness The You you've always wanted to be."

—Rod Smith, two-times Super Bowl NFL
Champion, author of *The Rod Effect*

"In his latest book, *The Potential Principle*, Mark inspires others to unlock their true potential. He emphasizes that the only limitation we have is the limitation we place upon ourselves. This book provides a framework and insights as to how to be the best version of you! Thank you, Mark, for always encouraging continuous improvement. You inspire us to embrace the journey!"

—Zoe Kane, senior director, Sun
Pharmaceutical Industries, Inc.

THE
Potential
PRINCIPLE

THE
Potential
PRINCIPLE

A Proven System

FOR CLOSING THE GAP BETWEEN HOW GOOD YOU ARE
AND HOW GOOD YOU COULD BE

Mark Sanborn

NELSON
BOOKS

An Imprint of Thomas Nelson

Published in Nashville, Tennessee, by Nelson Books, an imprint of Thomas Nelson. Nelson Books and Thomas Nelson are registered trademarks of HarperCollins Christian Publishing, Inc.

Published in association with Yates & Yates, www.yates2.com.

Thomas Nelson titles may be purchased in bulk for educational, business, fund-raising, or sales promotional use. For information, please e-mail SpecialMarkets@ThomasNelson.com.

Scripture quotations are taken from the Holy Bible, King James Version (public domain).

Any Internet addresses, phone numbers, or company or product information printed in this book are offered as a resource and are not intended in any way to be or to imply an endorsement by Thomas Nelson, nor does Thomas Nelson vouch for the existence, content, or services of these sites, phone numbers, companies, or products beyond the life of this book.

Library of Congress Cataloging-in-Publication Data

Names: Sanborn, Mark, author.
Title: The potential principle : a proven system for closing the gap between how good you are and how good you could be / Mark Sanborn.
Description: Nashville : Thomas Nelson, 2017.
Identifiers: LCCN 2016044059| ISBN 9780718093143 (hardback) | ISBN 9780718093167 (eBook)
Subjects: LCSH: Self-actualization (Psychology)
Classification: LCC BF637.S4 S253 2017 | DDC 650.1--dc23 LC record available at https://lccn.loc.gov/2016044059

Printed in the United States of America

17 18 19 20 21 LSC 10 9 8 7 6 5 4 3 2 1

To everyone who is committed to continually getting better and making the world around them better too.

Contents

CONTENTS

PART 1

Why You Should Improve

CHAPTER 1

The Potential Principle

Wealth, notoriety, place and power are no measure of
success whatever. The only true measure of success
is the ratio between what we might have done and
what we might have been on the one hand, and the
thing we have made of ourselves on the other.

—H. G. WELLS

In 1985 three-time Olympic athlete John Howard was at the
Bonneville Salt Flats, trying to set a new land speed record . . .
on a bicycle. Howard was not riding your dad's Schwinn. His
was a specially built bicycle. One turn of the pedals moved
the bike more than 110 feet. When Howard set the land speed
record, his monitored heart rate was 195 beats per minute. His
top speed? 152 miles per hour.

If you guessed that this is the top speed for riding a bicycle,
you'd be wrong. A decade later, a European beat Howard's best
by reaching a top speed of 161 miles per hour.

You might have little or no interest in bicycles or land speed records. That's not the point. What's important is this: We have no idea what is possible physically, mentally, or organizationally. Most of us far underestimate our own potential and the potential of others.

BEYOND EXPERIENCE

Even though I'm no mind reader, I can say with a high degree of confidence that you were at least surprised, if not shocked, that a human could ride a bicycle so fast. Nothing in the average person's experience with bicycles would suggest that anyone could ride one as fast as 150 miles per hour. *We've* never ridden a bicycle faster than 40, maybe 50 miles per hour. What's more, *most of us* have never been in a car that's gone faster than 110 or 120. Based on our experience—that is, *what we know*—most of us would guess the top speed for a bicycle is far slower than what's actually possible.

This means that sometimes our experience—our frame of reference—works against us. In this case our experience didn't lead to a complete failure—we didn't say 500 miles per hour. But we set a limit based on what we *thought was possible*, only to find out that we didn't have a clue. Of course, most of us aren't terribly bothered that we underestimated the land speed record of bicycles.

But what about when the subject is you and your potential? The hard truth is that we use the same deductive powers on ourselves that we used to determine the speed of the fastest bike ride. In fact, it's actually worse. My question about the top speed of a bicycle was meant to put your imagination to the test. But what if I had asked, "How fast could *you* ride a bicycle?"

Now your experience is working against you even more. Once again, I can't possibly know how fast you think you can ride a bicycle. But I can tell you one thing: Your answer is probably wrong. You can ride a bike much faster than you think.

Your imagination is limited because of your experience. Maybe that's why Einstein is purported to have said imagination is more important than knowledge, "for knowledge is limited to all we know and understand."

Most likely, in making your estimate you're afraid of being *unrealistic*: Perhaps you've been criticized for aiming too high or trying to accomplish too much in the past. Or maybe you failed to meet a goal you or your boss set, and the memory still stings. Whatever the reason, experience makes us set the bar a little lower—just a little lower, a little more, and a tad more. There. We can hit that speed.

Now forget about the bike.

How good could you be? How much better might you be than you are right now?

BETTER THAN YOUR BEST

This book isn't about doing the impossible, like defying gravity or flying with no equipment of any kind. I'm not saying you can—or should even try to—ride a bike faster than you've ever ridden one before. This book is about making your best better. It is focused on helping you improve in whatever areas you choose and becoming even better than you were before.

This book also isn't about achieving your dreams, whatever they might be. If you've always wanted to start a business, this book won't tell you how. Many readers may have already achieved their dreams: mastered the skill, run the marathon, started a successful business, or published a book. The message of this book, however, is this: *No matter how good you've become, you can become better.* No matter what you've done so far, you still haven't fulfilled your potential.

For some of us, doing something we've never tried or always wanted to do is an achievement in its own right. We do the thing, and then we move on. But do you ever move on from being a parent? Do you ever move on from having a career? Do you ever move on from living a meaningful life? These are pursuits without end. They don't have a finish line. You can't brush the dust off your hands and say, "Well, that was fun. What's next?"

Improvement in the important areas of your life can and should be an ongoing journey.

Consider this example: John isn't just any doctor. He's the chief cardiac surgeon at one of the best hospitals anywhere. This means that John is one of the best cardiac surgeons in the world. Patients and colleagues come to John when they have the toughest problem, the hardest case, the most formidable challenge. Although self-effacing and humble with others, John knows he's the best. To be a surgeon requires a certain confidence—a firm belief in your own talents. John has this. He *wants* the toughest cases, because he *knows* he is the best.

At this stage in his career John has two choices. One, he can believe that he has reached the highest pinnacle of professional success. With nothing left to prove to himself or others, John can rest assured that he will always be considered one of the best surgeons in the world. He can, as the saying goes, rest on his laurels.

Or two, John can challenge himself to become better than his best. He could strive to improve his already excellent skills and continue to be challenged and stimulated. But here is a question: When you're the best, who can help you get better? It's a daunting challenge. Why? Because John is the standard against which other surgeons compare themselves. He has no one ahead of him to emulate. To get better—to get closer to his true potential—he will have to raise the bar he's already set.

Consider this quote from one of the most popular movies of the last fifty years: "Gentlemen, you are the top 1 percent of all naval aviators—the elite. The best of the best. We'll make you better."[1] (Did you recognize the movie? It was *Top Gun*.)

I assume that if you're reading this, you are already good, perhaps even among the best, at what you do. So what's my job? To show you how to keep improving, to get closer to fulfilling your potential. Or, most accurately, *to make your best better*.

BETTER AT WHAT?

If you are a naval aviator, professional athlete, world-renowned surgeon, or movie star, I'm delighted you're reading this book. But most of us don't work in such rarefied fields. We're executives, vice presidents, CEOs, CFOs, directors, managers, salespersons; we're fathers, mothers, employees, friends, associates, peers; we're athletes, coaches, teammates, and mentors. This book is for all of us. In this book I make little distinction between, say, being the best president and being the best mother. What goes into making both better is the same.

And that raises the most basic question: Better at what? Better at what matters to you. Better at being someone whom others respect, emulate, and trust. Better at being someone who continues to improve and achieve. A person who motivates, challenges, and inspires others through his or her example. You may not have considered it, but these qualities and others define leadership; and they make up the little metrics that allow us to start gauging how and where we're actually getting better, actually reaching more of our potential.

You certainly can measure being better than your best in dollars: increased sales, revenue, and income. Those are legitimate metrics of success, and ones that you need to use to keep your job. I hope to show, however, that monetary improvement is usually the result of improving what you are already the best at.

As we'll see, the skills that people must improve to be better than their best are often different from the ones that got them to their current positions. While most people think about improving their jobs or performance skills, the more important thing to focus on is improving your mental, contemplative, and reflective skills. These are the metrics that can't be measured by employer evaluations, but they measure the skills that allow us to move beyond what we have ever thought was possible.

I can't teach John, our chief cardiac surgeon, about medicine or surgery. But I can teach the process that he or anyone else can use to improve. I can challenge his thinking and understanding and provide new insights he can then apply to his highly specialized area. And that's what we'll be doing in this book. Just as I have nothing to say to John about medicine, I'm unlikely to have anything to say to you about your profession. But in getting better than our best, whatever the thing is—the job, the hobby, the pursuit—is almost beside the point. The point is us. You. Me. If the goal is for *us* to be the ones to get better, then what needs to improve is inside of us.

UNLOCKING THE POTENTIAL

In the cognitive sciences there is a phenomenon known as the Pygmalion effect. Also known as the Rosenthal effect for one of the psychologists who discovered it, the phenomenon is simple enough: It reveals that higher expectations lead to better performance. The phenomenon is more than a theory; it has been demonstrated in the lab.

So why don't we expect more from ourselves? This can be especially difficult if we're already good (even the best) at something, since then we can have difficulty imagining how much better we could be.

The result is that we limit our expectations, which in turn is how we limit our disappointments. If we expect much, we are often disappointed. To avoid that, we lower our expectations. He or she who expects little and gets little is never disappointed.

One of the keys to continual improvement is the willingness to risk disappointment, to see disappointment not as a bad thing to be avoided but as proof positive we are aiming higher and striving to get better. I will go so far as to say that highly successful people are more often disappointed than are other people. They just don't let disappointment bother them.

So the questions become:

- How can you imagine a future even bigger than your past?
- How can you raise your sense of how fast you can ride a bicycle?
- How do you overcome the limitation of your experiences?
- How do you imagine yourself becoming better than you already are?

This book is about unlocking your imagination to pursue more of your potential. And when you do that, your best just keeps getting better.

CHAPTER 2

Why Get Better?

This is an interesting planet. It deserves
all the attention you can give it.

—MARILYNNE ROBINSON, *GILEAD*

Over the years I've worked with many companies and individuals who have told me that their goal was to become the best at what they did. They each wanted to be recognized as number one or the top in their field or industry. For some, the goal was only aspirational; for others, the goal was actually achieved.

Becoming "the best" is difficult indeed. It takes an intense focus and willingness to invest time, energy, and money that most people are either unwilling or unable to invest.

And there are no guarantees. You can labor for years and still find that reaching the pinnacle eludes you. But as difficult as it is to become the best, there is something even more difficult: *becoming the best and then continuing to get even better.*

BETTER ALWAYS BEATS BEST

There is only one thing that beats "best"—the best company, the best performer, the best accomplishment—and that is *better*.

Better. Better always beats best.

Better is an improvement. Better increases value and defeats complacency. Better moves us forward and makes "best" second best.

Everyone likes better: better relationships, better health, better jobs, better everything.

Have you ever heard anyone say, "Please, don't make it better"? I didn't think so.

Customers want better. They like it when they get more in the way of services, products, and benefits.

Our employers want better. They will not pay us more money simply to get more of the same performance. If we want to grow our earning potential, we must also grow the value we contribute to our company.

If you're an employer, a leader, or a manager, your employees and team members likely want better too. They want you to lead them a little better today than you did yesterday. They don't accept complacency in a boss any more happily than a boss accepts complacency in an employee.

What about at home? Wouldn't your spouse prefer a better relationship, regardless of how good it is now? Don't you think that after ten years of marriage, your relationship should be better than it was after ten weeks? We want love to grow, not to stagnate.

If you are not a better parent as you get older, you are not paying attention. If you want your kids to do better and better, you must set the pace and be the example.

In short, better is the ultimate strategy for succeeding in your professional life and in your personal life.

THREE REASONS TO GET BETTER PROFESSIONALLY

You need a compelling motivator to change any behavior. Among the best motivators is seeing the benefits that will result from making the change. The drive to pursue your potential will be more successful when you are clear on the benefits that effort will provide.

1. Customers

I blog with four great friends and colleagues—Joe Calloway, Scott McKain, Randy Pennington, and Larry Winget—and we periodically offer each of our perspectives on a specific topic.

Recently, we turned to this question: What is the biggest challenge business will face in the future? My response was ever-higher customer expectations. Not only do customers want more and ask for more; increasingly they demand and get more, or they go elsewhere.

That's the problem with being great: expectations are exceedingly high. We don't expect much from mediocre businesses, and when we don't get much, we aren't surprised. But when we do business with an elite organization, things are different: we have higher expectations, we are more sensitive to the experience, and we are more disappointed when we don't get what we expected.

If you aren't growing your value proposition and ability to deliver—in short, getting better—you are unlikely to be growing your customer base (unless you compete at the very low end of the market on price).

2. Competitors

Do you know why locust swarms move so fast? Each locust is trying to eat the locust in front of it.[1] And each locust is being pursued by a locust that wants to eat it. Fly faster and you get lunch; don't fly fast enough, you become lunch.

Doesn't that seem a lot like competition in the workplace today? You are trying to take market share from your competitors, and at the same time your competitors want to take market share from you.

You compete for a job promotion that another half dozen colleagues want as well. Or you interview for a new job at a different company with a plethora of candidates going for the same position.

I love what football coach Woody Hayes said while I was at Ohio State University: "You're either getting better or you're getting worse." In a world where everyone is competing, "status quo" is a myth. If you stay the same, you lose ground to those around you who are making their best better.

3. Change

What's the difference between science fiction and reality? Often just a matter of time. I was floored to read an article in the *Wall Street Journal* about head transplants being done in China. No, not on humans, but on mice. A leading surgeon there was able to transplant a head on a mouse that then lived for up to a day.[2] That may not be great news for the mice, but it boggles the imagination in terms of where medicine is headed and what in a matter of time may be possible.

Are there any "evergreen" businesses or industries left? What about driving a cab? There will always be a demand for cab drivers, right?

Along came Uber and upset the taxi apple cart. But prognosticators say that Uber and services like it don't have a long-term lock on providing transportation. NEVs (neighborhood electric vehicles) that are driverless may someday displace many vehicles driven by humans. And that likely explains Uber's recent efforts to acquire driverless cars. Smart companies—like smart people—look for potential threats that change creates and then try to make change work for them rather than against them.

In a world of constant change, you can't excel with only the skills of the past. Some of those skills need to be improved; some of them need to be replaced. And that's another terrific reason for making your best better.

LET'S GET PERSONAL

"Everyone has inside himself a piece of good news! The good news is that you really don't know how great you can be, how much you can love, what you can accomplish, and what your potential is!"

—ANNE FRANK

As we've just seen, there are many reasons why you need to get better professionally. But there are also compelling reasons why you need to get better personally.

Purpose

Why do you do what you do? Why do you get out of bed and head to work and go through life each day? One reason is habit, of course. Humans are habitual creatures who tend to go through the same motions day in and day out. Another reason is necessity: workplace compensation keeps our home life humming.

But let's not forget purpose. Purpose is the ultimate answer to the question of why you do what you do. Whether you know it or not, it's the reason you exist, your raison d'être.

How many Americans know their purpose? The Centers for Disease Control and Prevention says four out of ten have not discovered a satisfying life purpose.

My backup choice for a worldview comes from the existential school of philosophy. Existentialism is a belief that we live in an unfathomable world and that individuals are free and responsible for what they make of themselves. While no external purpose exists, the challenge is to create a purpose for yourself.

As a person of faith, however, I hold a worldview based on the belief that our lives have a purpose, one that is external to us and one that is less created by us than it is discovered by us. Whether or not you agree with my worldview, the challenge remains: How can you create or discover the purpose behind your activities and endeavors?

The better you become, the better you will be able to

fulfill your purpose. Only purposeful achievement is ultimately sustainable. Otherwise you risk concluding, *Since nothing ultimately matters, why try?*

Potential

> "The greatest waste in the world is the difference between what we are and what we could become."
>
> —Dr. Ben Herbster

Not long ago, I delivered a speech at a multinational electronics firm. Just before I took the stage, I congratulated the senior vice president of sales on the company's success. "Congrats," I said. "You and your team are leading your competitors in market share by a significant margin."

"Please don't say that onstage," he said, irritation in his voice. "We are leading in our industry, but we're not achieving to the level of our capabilities. We don't benchmark against our competitors. We benchmark against our capabilities."

What about you? You might be wildly successful, but are you living up to your true potential?

If you do indeed have a purpose, would it make sense for that purpose to include *not* living up to your true capabilities and potential?

I rarely meet people who believe they are realizing their true potential. I know I'm not. The problem is that we really don't know how good we can be. Many people I meet and work with readily acknowledge that they certainly could do more, accomplish more, be more.

It is exciting to wake up in the morning knowing that more

is possible. We should be grateful for what we have, what we've accomplished, and who we've become. But we should be just as grateful that we get another day to pursue our potential and find out how much better we could be.

People

Have you ever known someone who was so depleted—from lack of sleep, resources, health, or ambition—that he or she had nothing to offer others?

It's sad for people like this, and for those around them. It's a tough situation all around. At the same time, the most vibrant people I know are those whose lives are filled with enthusiasm, experiences, skills, and knowledge that make them rich resources and blessings to all those they encounter.

When you get better, people you live with and work with benefit too. The better you become, the more you have to contribute to others.

Furthermore, I believe that true success in life is about making the money necessary to fulfill our highest values, which are at the core of how we derive meaning in what we do.

JUST WHAT IS BETTER?

Who decides what is better? You do.

You will get better in those areas where you want to improve.

As you begin this process of improvement, you would be wise to consider input from people you live and work with.

Getting better at a skill that you may enjoy but that isn't important to your boss won't make you better at work. It may make you better in general terms, as well as happier, but to impress your boss, what you need to find is that important intersection between desired improvement and profitable improvement.

The same holds true for customers. Better products and services are voted on by those who buy them. An improvement that isn't important to your customer may be satisfying to you, but it won't increase revenues. I've had plenty of brilliant ideas. The problem is that my clients didn't always agree with me.

So, while you define better, in a practical sense better rarely happens in isolation. You live and work with others who are impacted by your improvement (or lack thereof). It only makes sense for you to include them as you consider your metrics for making your best better.

ONLY ONE THING CAN PREVENT YOU FROM GETTING BETTER

Recently I was working with a client on his presentation skills. He's not a professional speaker but is an executive with a commitment to continual improvement. He knows that the better he learns to communicate, the more effective he will be as a leader.

"I wish my boss would get some help from you on her presentation skills. She could be so much more effective. But it will never happen," my client shared.

Why?

"She doesn't think she needs any help."

You can't help those who don't think they need it. If you try, they will resist and likely resent you. The best teacher can help arouse desire for learning in a student, but he or she can't make a student learn. A great coach can inspire and teach, but only those willing to do the work will improve. A terrific leader can provide a compelling vision and the road map to achieve it, but a team member must be willing to take the journey.

I'm my own biggest obstacle. You are your biggest obstacle. As the pastor D. L. Moody once said, "I've had more trouble with myself than with any other man."

You've probably heard it said that most people are doing as well as they know how to do. I believe most people are doing *as well as they want to do*. Far more people know how they could improve, but they aren't willing to invest the time and energy to do it.

I had lunch with a friend who had just engaged a nutritionist to help him improve his health. I asked him how things were going. He said, "It was going terribly . . . until I decided to do the work." Like many, he had hoped working with a nutritionist would be enough. She helped change his thinking, but he still had to do the work and eat differently. The best information is worthless until you apply it.

My friend was proof that there is no silver bullet. No coach, mentor, counselor, consultant, employee, friend, parent, or spouse can do it for you. They can each encourage and assist you, but eventually you must do the work.

TWO PATHS TO IMPROVEMENT

There are two ways to get better: matrix improvement and breakthrough improvement.

Matrix improvement, as I'll reveal in the chapters ahead, means understanding the four areas of possible improvement: *thinking*, *performing*, *learning*, and *reflecting*. I'll explain the potential and pitfalls of each of those four areas and show you how you can apply breakthrough improvement in each of those areas. Matrix improvement is about focus and skill. Work on the four areas of your matrix and you will improve.

Breakthrough improvement comes from consistently using a small set of tools, steps that will prevent complacency, create improvement, and bust through barriers. These are the steps we each need to take:

1. Disrupt yourself (before someone else does).
2. (re)Focus.
3. Engage others.
4. Expand your capacity.

By combining matrix and breakthrough improvement and using both consistently and effectively, you will be squarely on the road to making your best better.

WHAT DO YOU WANT?

Before you can become better, you have to want to be better. I meet lots of people who are happy with the status quo. They are doing well enough and are content. Good for them. That's a far better place to be than being discontent. But for me—and I'm guessing you as well—complacency is not the path to take.

Survival and success require each of us to improve our game at some level. Failing to do so can result in the loss of opportunities or a diminished standard of living. You can frame that reality as a depressing duty or as an incredible opportunity. I choose to do the latter.

Any of us can get better at anything if we truly desire to improve. We might never be the best, but we can always better our best. And that counts for a lot.

Wouldn't you like to find out just how good you can be?

Together, let's follow the potential principle and find out how to narrow the gap between how good you are and how good you could be.

HOW I GET BETTER

Joe Calloway, Consultant, Speaker, and Author

I see curiosity as being a skill for improvement, and I develop and exercise my own curiosity as I would any other skill. I read articles, books, newspapers, and websites about subjects that, on the surface, might seem to have nothing to do with my work, career, or life. But what these seemingly random sources do for me is spark ideas that lead me down paths on which I discover new perspectives about the world. I exercise my curiosity in this way just as intentionally as I exercise my body at the gym. My curiosity leads me to new ways of thinking, which lead me to become better at what I do.

PART 2

The Path to Improvement

CHAPTER 3

The Potential Matrix

True happiness involves the full use
of one's power and talents.

—John Gardner

I grew up using paper maps. Unfolding them was easy. Refolding them was hard. But the information they provided was crucial. When you were planning a trip, the first thing you went to was a good map.

The value of a map isn't just in showing how to reach your destination. A map also shows you what you can see along the way. And like many things in life, the route you choose depends on what you want to experience. Do you want a shorter path from A to B that strategically enhances efficiency, or a longer path that allows you to see and experience more—to linger? Do you want to take the highway or hit the back roads? Are charming small towns your thing, or do you want to pass through exciting cities?

Over the years I've developed a map of sorts that shows you how to reach your potential. This "map" is more accurately described as a matrix divided into four quadrants that are crucial to your journey toward improvement.

As we will see, this type of four-quadrant representation offers a practical way to think about the experience of leadership and growth. It will help you make sense of the journeys you have taken (and those you haven't). As you surely have learned over the years, the routes you can choose to take to any destination are nearly countless. And yet, what's fascinating is that most people stick with only one route, depriving themselves of the variety and creativity that come from trying different paths.

THE BENEFITS OF USING THE POTENTIAL MATRIX

The Potential Matrix does the following:

1. *It provides a proven path to improvement*, regardless of how good you already are. Familiarity with the four quadrants isn't enough; instead, we'll focus on optimizing each quadrant to the degree that's necessary for *you*.
2. *It enables us to make full use of our spectrum of resources and skills.* One key thing to know about this simple map: you aren't currently using all four areas—or more specifically, you're overusing one or more area and underusing the others. Overuse and underuse translate into room for improvement.
3. *It leverages each of the other quadrants.* Each area complements the others. If you are headed toward better,

you'll want to use each of the four areas identified. Doing so will help you reach your destination sooner and, perhaps more important, enrich the trip.

4. *It uncovers critical insights that will help you understand yourself better.* For example, leveraging learning with reflection or leveraging performance with thinking will give you new insights about yourself and the world in which we live.

THE INNER/OUTER DILEMMA

In more than thirty years of working with leaders from corporations, philanthropies, churches, the government sector, and academia, I've noticed a pronounced split in people between their outer worlds of doing and their inner worlds of being.

Let's look at a couple of examples.

Marissa is a C-level exec who has achieved significant professional success—promotions and praise—at the technology company where she works. She isn't a fan of the company's owner, and the company itself isn't anything to write home about—better products are on the market, no question. But profits are good, and her overall workplace and her job are fine. In fact, she earns a mid-six-figure income and quarterly bonuses. Better yet, she's happily married with two wonderful children and finds the time to stay fit and healthy.

And yet Marissa is undergoing a crisis. Lately she has been asking herself what difference, if any, her work makes—to her or to anyone else, for that matter. Sure, she has a good salary, but beyond that she's at a loss. Despite her success in meeting challenges at work, she feels unfulfilled and dissatisfied, almost as if she's killing time to earn a killer paycheck.

Greg is the pastor of a church of eight hundred. He entered ministry because of his deeply held convictions. He earned an advanced degree in biblical studies and has a rich inner life. But his church's growth has plateaued. Throughout his career, Greg has had a difficult time in matters of administration, preaching, and leadership. He has been unsuccessful in forming staff and volunteer teams and has struggled with expressing the beliefs he holds so sacred.

What's going on with Marissa and Greg?

Let's start with Marissa. Some leaders like Marissa are great at doing. They excel at doing their jobs, learn quickly, run organizations, keep the corporate engine humming, and create tangible results. But if you start to explore their inner worlds, you'll find they've spent far less time—and are often far less comfortable—dealing with questions of purpose and significance.

As Gordon MacDonald has said, "Most of us prefer to do our business at the surface. We invest the preponderant amount of our energies out there where we can see what is going on, where mystery is cut to the minimum, where people take notice and reward us."

On the other hand, pastors like Greg often have the most developed inner lives I've observed. Their focus is on delving deeply into matters of purpose, motives, character, and integrity. They work to understand the private life of the heart, mind, and soul. What people like Greg often lack is a greater focus on the outer world of business (even pastors have a job to do, and most take that job seriously). In Greg's case, he could benefit from learning how to communicate more effectively, lead teams, develop training programs, and administer a thriving organization.

If not acknowledged and addressed, this tendency to fixate almost exclusively on one world—inner or outer—can be a tremendous liability. Many highly successful people are unsatisfied because they don't really know what difference their efforts make. Many introspective, contemplative people, in turn, are unable to effectively communicate their belief systems, knowledge, and experiences in a way that will truly impact others.

That's where the opportunity lies—Marissa and Greg can get better and be better at a world that is foreign to them. And the Potential Matrix is a way to make that happen.

The Potential Matrix

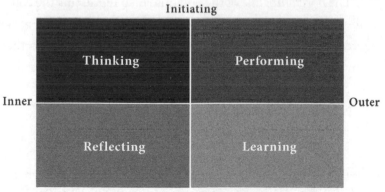

THE POTENTIAL MATRIX

It's important to understand the geography of getting better. For starters, in the Potential Matrix above, there's a vertical and a horizontal line.

The *vertical line* represents the action mode of getting better. Perhaps one of the greatest illusions about improvement is that it's based solely on what you initiate on your own. This is what is found at the top of the vertical line. But there is often more to improvement than simply what is found at the top of that line. A significant component of bettering your best actually involves waiting, observing, listening, and learning, which are found at the base of the vertical line.

The initiating-responding continuum includes activities such as observing and listening (at the base of the vertical line), along with interactive, collaborative activities involving a great deal of effort and attention, such as speaking, planning, motivating, and team building (at the top of the line).

The *horizontal line* of the potential map represents the continuum from inner to outer worlds. The left side of the axis represents the inner world unseen to others but known to the individual (where Greg lives). The right side happens in the company or community of others (Marissa's world).

Now, let's break down the quadrants.

Performing Quadrant

This is the quadrant familiar to most people. It's where most of us consciously spend each day *doing things*: the observable world of initiating, acting, and producing. Performing is what we are expected to do when we show up to work each day.

Though it may go without saying, not everyone who is busy is productive. Activity and results aren't the same thing. Those who look busy but accomplish little are simply posing and posturing. They're going through the motions.

Learning Quadrant

It takes effort to learn. But in a way, ideas act on us if we seek them out and are receptive to them. Learning new ideas can lead to skills development, more concrete thinking, and deeper reflection. Most often we associate learning as a precursor to performance.

But what of those who keep learning without any real application of the information they glean? A person who has several graduate-level degrees but no job might be described as a dabbler, one who acquires ideas rather than implementing or acting on them.

Thinking Quadrant

Thinking is about proactively contemplating the world around you. It's the source of vision, dreams, plans, and strategies. It uses external input and creates connections and directions.

Some people, however, never leave the space inside their heads. They are the daydreamers, people full of big ideas but unwilling to act.

Thinking done well, however, allows you to make sense of the world and create the world that could be.

Reflecting Quadrant

The lower left-hand quadrant, the inner world of responding, is, well, troublesome. It's the aspect of leadership that is least often considered, and—you can be the judge at the end of this book—probably the most important. In my experience, it's also the most difficult area. I call this dimension "the reflecting." The best words to describe this area are *waiting* and *listening*, not to others, but to God.

As we will see later, this area can be likened to an unusual space. Think of it as a room with no obvious entrance. While the room isn't inaccessible, most people find it challenging to enter. The leaders I've worked with often react to the idea of reflection in one of two ways: they never realized the room was there (because they have never entered), or they know about the room but consciously or unconsciously choose not to spend much time there.

As with any of the four quadrants, if you linger here too long, you will become stuck. Navel gazers sometimes reflect so deeply that they become paralyzed and cannot engage with the outer world.

TIPS FOR THE IMPROVEMENT JOURNEY

Using the Potential Matrix will narrow the gap between how good you are and how good you can be. It is a simple graphic, but it is rich with opportunity. Here are some ways to maximize your journey.

Combat Comfort to Overcome Complacency

One reason we don't get better is that we avoid the areas where we have greatest opportunities for improvement. It is human nature to focus on those areas in which we excel (or at least that are most comfortable). A strength used exclusively or overused can become a weakness. As one example, having highly developed presentation skills isn't helpful if you don't have anything important to say. One of the reasons I don't play golf—among many—is that I'm only good on short shots. But lacking the ability to drive the ball, I don't get many short shots. Because I'm not willing to improve my tee, fairway, and bunker shots, I miss many opportunities to get on the green with friends and associates.

Movement Equals Improvement

Look at the Potential Matrix again, and consider it as you read the following scenario.

The Potential Matrix

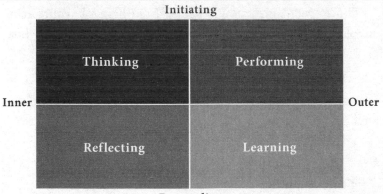

Imagine you have an important meeting coming up. Will you show up unprepared? Will you act bored, listen poorly, and engage as little as possible? Or on the flip side, will you dominate the conversation and ignore other points of view?

While it's true that some meetings are definitely more frustrating than others, I hope you don't adopt any of the behaviors just described. Rather, you should work through the potential map before and during the meeting. You should *think* about the agenda in advance and *reflect* upon what has gone well and what has not in past meetings. Maybe you'll *do* some preparation in order to *learn* about each of the participants, their points of view, and their roles in the upcoming discussion. Then at the meeting you'll contribute ideas, facilitate the sharing of ideas, and be an effective listener.

Your ability to move among the four quadrants will greatly affect your participation in the meeting and the degree of success you experience in it.

The Long Route to Better

Since each area complements the other, ask yourself a simple question: How can one, two, or all three of the other areas help me right now where I am today?

The direct route—investing in just one area—while the fastest, is the most limiting. You can become only so good at any of the four areas before you must use the others to improve.

Balance Isn't the Point

I've been using the Potential Matrix for nearly twenty years, and I don't distribute my time equally in each of the four areas. My four areas aren't perfectly balanced; instead, they're perfectly imbalanced. For example, I can tell which areas are most appropriate to focus on in light of the current challenge or need, and I easily identify which areas I'm neglecting.

The Potential Matrix is a guide, or a map. Maps are tools. They show us new places we may not have previously seen or considered. And they provide possible routes to get us from where we are to where we want to be. But a map doesn't make us do anything. A map doesn't direct; it simply suggests. We still must choose our courses, and choosing well determines the quality of our journeys. The Potential Matrix will keep you focused on where and how to improve.

In the next four chapters, you'll learn more about each of the four quadrants in the Potential Matrix, and how to use them for consistent improvement.

Actions

1. Don't linger in your quadrant of greatest comfort.
2. Move frequently and freely between the quadrants for maximum growth.
3. Use each quadrant to leverage the benefits you gain from the others.
4. Remember: don't pursue balance; pursue better.

HOW I GET BETTER

Ken Philbrick, Partner and Owner of
Adam James International

I get better by humbling myself, seeking wisdom, and putting my clients' interests over mine. In order to gain wisdom, I humbly ask God to help me, and then read the book of Proverbs. I surround myself with a few close friends and mentors who challenge me and hold me accountable. They understand my strengths and weaknesses and help me become a better husband, father, friend, and businessman.

As an extreme extrovert, I have struggled throughout my life to be an effective listener. I have taken to heart the lesson from *The Fred Factor* whereby it is more important to be interested than interesting. When I meet with a client, I work hard to actively LISTEN and let the other person TALK. By always putting the other person first and sincerely caring for his or her business and personal success, I have become an effective partner to my clients.

CHAPTER 4

Escalating Performance

If You Don't Think You Can Keep Getting Better, You Don't Know Jack

Be so good they can't ignore you.

—STEVE MARTIN

The Potential Matrix

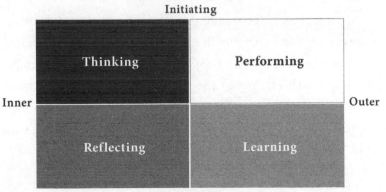

Fitness legend Jack LaLanne changed his life when, as a teenager, he heard a nutritionist speak. Soon thereafter, he gave up sugar. He subsequently opened the first fitness club in the United States and starred in his own TV show, which aired for thirty years.

LaLanne was highly disciplined in every aspect of his life. He followed a strict diet and exercised two hours daily: one hour of strength training and one hour of swimming. He became known as "the godfather of fitness."[1]

A great showman and salesman, he used stunts of physical prowess—like doing 1,033 push-ups in twenty-three minutes—to promote his business. In 1974, at the age of sixty, LaLanne swam in the San Francisco Bay from Alcatraz Island to Fisherman's Wharf. And he did so handcuffed and shackled while towing a one-thousand-pound boat.

At age sixty-five, he towed sixty-five boats in a lake near Tokyo, Japan. Again he was handcuffed and shackled, and this time the boats were filled with sixty-five hundred pounds of wood pulp.

At age seventy, he was handcuffed, shackled, and fighting strong winds and currents in Los Angeles as he towed seventy rowboats holding seventy people from the Queen's Way Bridge in Long Beach Harbor to the *Queen Mary*, docked one mile away. The water temperature ranged from sixty to seventy degrees. It took him two hours. Afterward he said that he was cold, but had never thought of quitting.

Jack LaLanne never stopped getting better.

WHY KEEP GETTING BETTER?

If you've already achieved a certain level of success, you may think there's little need to try to improve. But you couldn't be more mistaken. Here's why.

1. Getting Better Is Primarily How Others Evaluate You at Work and in Other Situations

What you think, believe, and aspire to are important, but they are rendered useless unless coupled with action. And action, improved over time, creates a performance that proves your worth.

2. Getting Better Creates the Results You Desire

Just as the proof is in the performance, so is the payoff. Competitive advantage, career advancement, closed sales, and loyal employees are just a few of the results a better performance generates.

3. Getting Better Is Observable and Easy to Track

How well you think, reflect, or even learn are far less obvious than how you perform. And the only thing better than a standout performance is the better thinking, reflecting, and learning that support it.

4. Getting Better Is Proof of Improvement

This is how you truly know you've bettered your best. If your future performance surpasses your present and past performance, you are on the rise.

WHY SATISFACTORY
STUNTS IMPROVEMENT

Every day we "perform," at work and at home, in ways big and small. Because we can't (and shouldn't) give every performance the same attention, it is easy to be lulled into a sense that satisfactory is good enough.

To keep getting better at the important performances of your life, you need a new mind-set:

Satisfactory is anything but.

In the trivial things, satisfactory is enough. But making your best better means that satisfactory is insufficient; it is the low threshold to benchmark against.

But perfection isn't the point either.

Whenever you aim for perfection, you attain something less, but what you attain is significantly better than what you previously had done.

The point is improvement—knowing that for practical purposes, ultimate performance is either unknown or unattainable. Many people become discouraged when they try to improve and still turn in imperfect performances.

George Leonard, in his classic book *Mastery*, pointed out that improvement isn't a linear, upward-sloping line but rather a series of stair steps. You improve, keep working, but plateau temporarily.[2] It seems as if you are not getting better, when suddenly—and often unpredictably—another improvement occurs.

Mark your progress over time, looking for periodic but identifiable improvements. Aim beyond satisfactory, and you will move increasingly toward your potential.

THREE "SECRETS" TO IMPROVING YOUR PERFORMANCE

The ideas I'm about to share aren't secrets in the strictest sense of the word. But few, it seems, consider and use these ideas to better their best.

First, Performance Improves When You Enjoy It

Here's a rhetorical question: Do you perform better when you are enjoying yourself? Of course you do. You might suffer through a performance that is stellar, but that is rare. A superb performance isn't just about what you do, how well you do it, or what others think. It is about how you feel when you are doing it.

What is the point of better performance if you don't feel better too?

Play is innately creative. Rigid rules and structure will help you develop your foundation, but play is what brings artistry to your performance.

This doesn't mean you will enjoy the preparation, practice, or even every performance. But when you can find and focus on what you enjoy and are good at, your improvement will come much easier.

Second, Dedication and Discipline Are Twins

If you say you are dedicated, you are also speaking indirectly of your willingness to do what needs to be done, and that is discipline. Discipline, as I define it, is the ability to do what needs to be done even when you don't feel like it.

Anything of value will require discipline, and lack of it is the chief enemy of better.

Third, Remember That the Best Have Already Created a Path for You

We have an example in the way they lived their lives and ran their businesses that helps guide us in achieving similar success.

Rare is the innovator who knew little and then created much. In earlier times apprenticeship was about working for a master to learn your craft or trade. You emulated the master to develop the necessary skills.

As I share in my other books and tell my clients, you first emulate to learn, but then innovate to earn. You can only break the rules when you know what the rules are. You can only innovate when you deeply understand what is already being done and then do it differently.

HOW TO BOOST YOUR PERFORMANCE

1. Use FIT to Better Your Best Performance

You know practice is important, but how important, and what makes practice effective?

Anders Ericsson, the author of *Peak: Secrets from the New Science of Expertise*, has pointed out that Malcom Gladwell, in his book *Outliers*, didn't exactly get the ten-thousand-hour rule right (and I referenced it myself in one of my previous books). It isn't just about the amount of practice, but the kind of practice that creates improvement. Ericsson says, "In pretty much any area of human endeavor, people have a tremendous capacity to improve their performance, as long as they train in the *right way* . . . You can keep going and going, getting better and better and better. How much you improve is up to you." [3]

The key? What Ericsson calls "deliberate practice" is a highly structured activity engaged in with the specific goal of improving performance: "We have found no limitations to the improvements that can be made with particular types of practice."[4]

For years I've exercised five or six days a week. For me, the minimum effective dose is enough to maintain health and energy. Sometimes I've become discouraged that I wasn't improving. After consideration, I realized this was the result of something wrong in one or more of these three categories, which together go by the acronym FIT.

Frequency: The more often you do something correctly, the better you will become. You'll go from incompetence to competence by adding more practice.

Showing up is a start—though as you'll see soon, it's just a start. The more you do anything, the more reasonably you can expect improvement (unless you are just going through the motions).

Intensity: The energy, focus, and attention you bring to the performance of a task determine how well you perform it. Just as lifting light weights in the gym has a different outcome than pressing heavy weights, so does the amount of effort you bring to what you are doing.

I've observed people exercising by doing a set of six to eight repetitions of a movement followed by ten minutes of texting. While it is good that they showed up to exercise, they won't be experiencing much, if any, improvement for one reason: they lack intensity.

Technique: If your technique is wrong or suboptimal, frequency and intensity will only make matters worse. The gym is a great example of well-meaning people doing incorrect or even dangerous things. The wrong technique can result in energy drain and set back improvement.

Good performance is about great technique. Better performance is about learning better techniques. And it follows that if you want to be truly great, you use the techniques developed and employed by the truly great.

2. Use Feedback

Feedback is information you can use to improve your performance. It often comes from others, but it also can be accomplished through your own thoughtful analysis.

Effective feedback comes from people who understand what you are doing, what you did wrong, and what you could do better. But don't confuse feedback with opinion. When I give a speech, audience members often share what they liked, or didn't like, or wish I had done. And some of the ideas are helpful. Usually, however, they are personal opinions.

If there is an accomplished professional speaker or communication coach in the audience, he or she can provide me with feedback. This professional's knowledge is proven, and he or she looks at an onstage performance as a mechanic looks at an engine, not preferring what the engine looked like, but knowing how the engine could be better tuned.

Have you heard someone say, "I am my own worst critic"?

People who say this generally mean that they are tougher on their own performance than others are. Self-criticism seems positive on the surface, but it doesn't help. If anything, it hinders. It results in feeling bad about your performance but doesn't mean you learn what you can do to make it better.

Instead of being your own worst critic, be your own best evaluator. Process whatever emotion you need to work through, and then become analytical: What worked? (Do more of it.) What didn't work? (Understand why.) What could have worked better? (Figure out how.) These are questions that will lead you to useful information.

3. Codify Your Performance

When you codify something, you arrange the rules in systematic order. That makes them easier to remember and easier to use. It creates powerful consistency too.

Jack LaLanne codified his entire life, from what he ate to when he ate it to when and how long he worked out. He brought the same focus to bear on his business ventures as well.

One reason performance is often hit or miss is that on a good day we remember and use the rules. On a bad day we forget to use a few.

The Checklist Manifesto was a bestselling book about how checklists can be used to dramatically reduce errors and increase discipline in personal and organizational performance. The author, Atul Gawande, is a surgeon who drew upon his own and other surgeons' experience to improve surgical outcomes.[5]

Pilots use checklists too. Most professionals who are consistent use checklists of some kind. They codify what needs to happen before, during, and after an important performance. Usually these checklists are written (in the case of pilots, they always are). But over time they can become mental.

I've developed my own checklists and abbreviations for improvement in many areas of my life. For instance, I found I often purchased things I didn't need. To simplify my life and stop wasting money, I start with UWYH: Use What You Have. Is there something I already possess that would serve the needed purpose? If so, I use that first. In all areas of business, I use the simple concept PP: Prepare Powerfully. I've found that anything from a conversation to a meeting, to a speech to a sales call, can be significantly improved through powerful preparation, which is preparation beyond what others are willing to make.

4. Track Your Progress

A critical question for bettering your performance is this: How will you know when you've been successful?

An effective self-evaluation is more than feedback from others. It is also a measure to track progress or regress. You might think that anecdotal comments are proof of getting better. But that's not necessarily the case. People, perhaps especially well-meaning ones, say nice things because they like you. Additionally, they rarely know what your performance looked like previously.

So, you need to use your present abilities as your baseline. And then look forward: What measure, tools, assessments, or instruments could you use that would give you valuable information about your improvement?

THE BEST PERFORMANCE EVERY TIME

Not every action you take, behavior you apply, or performance you give will be the best ever given by anyone anywhere. That is strictly impossible. Even the greatest at their craft can't sustain that kind of ideal performance. There is sometimes an element of inexplicable mystery to those kinds of amazing performances.

Many years ago, Sir Laurence Olivier gave a performance that was, even for him, extraordinary. When a friend went backstage to congratulate him, he found the actor in a foul mood. "What's wrong?" the friend wanted to know. "That was one of the most incredible performances I've ever seen."

Olivier replied, "Yes, but I don't know how I did it."

Even the greats don't always completely understand all that creates a record-setting or award-winning performance. There is no guaranteed formula for ultimate performance.

But even though Olivier wasn't able to explain this "best-ever" achievement, he was still able to consistently deliver incredible acting performances.

The goal, of course, is to deliver the best performance you are capable of when it matters. Escalating performance is about practicing your craft so that each time you need to perform, your skills are a little better and your skill set is a little larger. Escalating your performance is more than an intention; it is about being willing to invest in getting better each day.

Make your next performance your best performance every time.

Actions

1. Focus on FIT: frequency, intensity, and technique.
2. Practice as often as you can.
3. Ask for feedback and create your own.
4. Track your progress.

HOW I GET BETTER

John D. Bledsoe, Financial Consultant,
CFP, CLU, ChFC, MSFS, AEP, EIEIO

I get better in my practice of working with the mega-wealthy by carefully observing the outcome of my prospect and client encounters. The questions I ask are in a very specific order and asked in a specific way learned through my observations of the thousands of these that I have done. The most effective results are gained by my repressing my particular tastes and attitudes toward the subject and focusing only on what the client's feelings are about each subject. If I have a great fact-finding meeting, then the next meeting, with my specific recommendations, is very easy. I have an exact presentation of solutions that is custom fit to the people I am meeting with. I plan on getting better and better for as long as I am alive, and it requires my full attention to detail and the strong desire to believe that good enough is not good enough.

CHAPTER 5

Leveraged Learning

How to Go from Waiting Tables to NASA

The people who make it remain teachable all
their lives. They keep trying to see better.

—ERWIN MCMANUS

The Potential Matrix

Initiating

Thinking	Performing
Reflecting	Learning

Inner

Outer

Responding

What keeps you from learning? Do you ever find yourself, as I sometimes do, bemoaning a lack of time or opportunity to pursue further or higher education?

Neither of those prevented a thirty-five-year-old working mother of three from making the move from waitress to NASA.[1]

Thirteen years ago, Cristine Andes was waiting tables to support her family. Because of her commitment to her marriage, her kids, and her job, she felt that life around her "just happens. I exist in a reactionary state of mind."

What changed? She made time to learn.

Today, after having completed three two-year degrees with honors and graduating summa cum laude with a 4.0 GPA and a bachelor of science in occupational safety and health, Cristine works at NASA as a quality assurance specialist.

How did she achieve these milestones?

She said, "I decided to go to a community college for a two-year degree in office administration. But even the decision to go to college was not an easy one. It meant taking on being a full-time student while working full-time and raising three boys with some family support and backing."

It wasn't easy for Cristine, and achievement isn't easy for most people. But highly successful people are more concerned with their growth than with their comfort. They are more committed to learning than to leisure.

"If I—a waitress and mother of three—can sit here thirteen years later and be in awe of what I do every day, anything is possible. All you need is faith, family support, and belief in yourself to make things happen."

Learning unlocks your potential. It is the superhighway to better.

WHY LEARN?

If you didn't have teachers who instilled a love of wonder and learning when you first started school, or parents who encouraged discovery and explanation, you might never have considered the real payoffs of learning. Here are a few.

1. Learning Can Help Break Through the Status Quo

You will get better when you have new and better things to do and consistently do them. Repeating what you are already doing just maintains your current level of performance. So you must keep learning. If you don't, you won't have any fuel for your improvement engine.

2. Learning Enables You to Benefit from the Wisdom of the Ages

Anyone can learn from the greatest men and women who ever lived. The ability to access information about their lives and lessons is easy, thanks to the Internet.

And unless you want to do so, you don't have to conduct primary research. If you want to learn something, lots of others have already done the hard work and written or recorded their findings. All that great information is available to you if you know where to look.

3. Learning Adds to Your Intellectual Arsenal

Our brains are far more capable of learning, remembering, and accessing information than we consider. While white noise, distraction, and stress might create the illusion that our brains are "full," that is never the case. The more you learn, the more you have to draw from for solving problems, generating creative solutions, and making novel connections.

4. Learning Doesn't Just Make You Better: It Keeps You Current

An expert who isn't learning won't remain an expert. As the world changes, so do the demands made on us. You don't have to learn everything, but you do need to continue to learn the things relevant to your career and life.

WE ARE ALL PERPETUAL NEWBIES

Kevin Kelly is a seminal thinker on matters of technology and their impact on us. In his book *The Inevitable*, he wrote, "No matter how long you have been using a tool, endless upgrades make you into a newbie—the new user often seen as clueless. In this era of 'becoming,' everyone becomes a newbie. Worse, we will be newbies forever. That should keep us humble."[2]

Kelly's premise is built on the fact that technology continually changes. But it isn't—and wasn't—technology alone that made us perpetual newbies. Learners have always known that new discoveries, insights, and inventions hold the potential to impact us at a personal level, and most eventually do. In a sense, Kelly was talking about what we've always been—perpetual newbies—but perhaps didn't realize it. And to a learner, that is exciting news.

LEVERAGED LEARNING BEGINS WITH A MIND-SET

You've heard how important attitude is to success, but what about mind-set? Turns out, it is essential for anyone who wants to get better.

Carol Dweck is a psychologist who has identified two different mind-sets that people possess: a fixed mind-set and a growth mind-set.

Those with a fixed mind-set believe that genetics primarily determine abilities; that is, intelligence and talents are inherited more than developed. As a result, these people fear failing because doing so makes them appear in their own eyes as incompetent, or worse, unintelligent or talentless. A fixed mind-set thus severely limits the ability to learn.

In contrast, people with a growth mind-set believe they can always get better through learning, work, and practice. They aren't discouraged by failure, and they analyze errors so they can learn from them. Regardless of how good they've become, they believe better is always possible.

In my work, I often come across both types of mind-sets. Recently, I overheard a conversation in an airport between two businessmen comparing the state of their companies. "I've gotten to a pretty good place," one of them said. "But I'm realistic. I'm not going to get smarter as I get older. My dad was in the same business, and he taught me what he knew, and I've used that and expanded on it. But I don't see how I can be any better than I am now."

His companion did not agree. "Are you kidding?" he replied. "I was never the smartest person in the room, and I don't think that way. I'm always looking for new ways to improve my business—and myself, for that matter. Does that mean everything I do succeeds? I wish. But some of it does, and that motivates me to learn more and try new things. I don't see myself ever stop trying to make things better. My motto is, what's next?"

Growth begins with a mind-set that better is not only possible, but also achievable through hard work. If you don't believe you can improve—no surprise here—you won't. You'll stay in your comfort zone, where you will be limited by your own thinking.

How comfortable is that?

WHY YOU'LL WANT TO BE AN AUTODIDACT

Years ago, I read a book by Charles Hayes called *Self University*, and I've since read several of his other books and writings. Hayes is an autodidact—that is, a self-taught person—and his business, Autodidactic Press, is dedicated to two propositions. The first is that lifelong learning is fundamental to living a full and interesting life. The second is that the learning necessary to gain competence in a job or career is far more important than *how* or *where* it is acquired.

Charlie Munger, one of the wealthiest and most respected

investors in the world, once said to a roomful of law school graduates, "Without lifetime learning you people are not going to do very well. You are not going to get very far in life based on what you already know. You're going to advance in life by what you're going to learn after you leave here . . . If civilization can progress only when it invents the method of invention, you can progress only when you learn the method of learning."[3]

To start your journey as an autodidact, I recommend two things.

First, take responsibility for learning how to learn. A paper published in *Psychological Science in the Public Interest* evaluated ten contemporary techniques for improving learning.[4] Of the ten, the average person scored low on five, moderate on three, and high on two. That suggests that most of us haven't come close to maximizing our ability to learn. You may study hard, but because you lack the right learning techniques, you know far less than you would have if you knew how to learn well.

Second, develop a learning agenda. I work with high-level leaders and am constantly amazed but no longer surprised by how few keep a formal learning agenda. Once you graduate from high school or college, you lose the benefit of a curriculum. A learning agenda is about identifying what you need to learn and then finding the time and resources to do it.

BEING TEACHABLE IS OVERRATED

Don't just be teachable. Be intentional.

We live in a learning-rich environment, but that doesn't

necessarily mean that the lessons are sticking. Structured learning is largely egalitarian and available to all, but not everyone takes advantage of the opportunities to learn.

It is easy to think that we're learning as we go, but in reality we are often just gathering experiences and extracting little in the way of lessons.

Being teachable means being open and receptive to learning. But it is passive. The student waits for the teacher to come. Active learning requires intentionality, and if you don't make it an overt objective in your journey, it won't happen consistently. Someone once said that for a lesson to make an impact, you have to understand what happened. That's true, and active learners work to try to understand.

Teachable people are open to others giving them lessons that will hopefully stick. Intentional learners look for the lessons that cascade through their lives daily.

WAYS TO LEVERAGE YOUR LEARNING

1. Build on the Basics

I've never liked the colloquialism "back to the basics." After all, who wants to go backward to get ahead?

I much prefer "building on the basics." Learning is highly cumulative: you build on and add to what you've already learned and then make new connections and discover fresh ideas.

What can happen is that you forget or ignore the fundamental lessons that, if missing, prevent your improvement. You need to periodically refresh and rehearse what you've learned. By reexamining the basics, you can tell what might have changed, what may have been disproved, or what is in need of updating.

2. Focus First on Learning What Is Relevant, Needed, and Necessary

It is easier to learn what you are interested in and enjoy. There should always be room in your learning agenda for those things. Just don't let what you *want* to learn displace what you *need* to learn.

A new system at work, revised regulations by your community association, and changed processes for travel might be mundane at some level but are still necessary to learn. So ask yourself what things are relevant to your job, your situation, or your advancement. Go beyond the merely interesting to the informative, which is information you can apply.

Also ask yourself what would happen if you inquired of your manager, coworker, spouse, or friend, "What do you think I most need to learn right now?" What would he or she say? Improvement at work and at home can begin with a question like this.

3. Review for Retention

Remember as a kid when you had to know the capital of every state in the United States to pass a test? How many capitals can you remember today? If you are like most people, you probably remember only a few of them. At the time of the test, you may have been able to provide their names, but you hadn't truly learned them. If you had, you would have retained that knowledge.

My greatest weakness as a learner is exactly this problem. I am a huge accumulator of ideas from a broad range of sources.

I capture lots of information, make many notes, and am well organized. My weakness is that I don't review as much as I could. What I need to remember is this equation:

$$capture + review = retention$$

Lately I've spent more time combing through notes, re-visiting lessons, and discarding outdated thinking. It has been a gratifying and productive time.

Try this exercise: Pick an area of professional or personal interest. Write down the ten most important lessons you've learned about that area of interest. Another variation is to pick a mentor or an influence from your life and write down the ten most important things you learned from him or her. This mental rehearsal will bolster the good ideas you've captured in the past, and you'll find new opportunities to apply them.

4. Teach It to Really Know It

Richard Feynman was many things, foremost a world-changing scientist and teacher. He was also a skilled explainer. Shane Parrish—the founder of *Farnam Street*, one of my favorite blogs—refers to a learning practice called the "Feynman Technique" as "the best way to learning anything." Here's how Parrish explains it:

1. Choose a concept.
2. Teach it to a toddler.
3. Identify the gaps and go back to the source material.
4. Review and simplify.

Being asked to explain something can uncover how little or how much you know about it. Asking you to teach something you think you understand to a toddler may seem silly, but as Parrish has pointed out, "When I used to learn new subjects I would explain them with complicated vocabulary and jargon. The problem with this approach is that I was fooling myself. I didn't know that I didn't understand."[5] Using the impressive words may allow you to bluff others, but it doesn't mean you have a full understanding.

When you find out what you don't know and can't explain well in trying to teach a topic, use those gaps so you'll know what you need to review or expand. You already know that review is good for retention, and simplification means being able to remove everything unnecessary but not too much.

Few things are as satisfying as learning something of value and being able to teach it to another.

5. Apply What You Know

Pretend, for a moment, that you are diagnosed with a life-threatening ailment. After finding the most successful doctor in the world in treating this condition, you wait months to get an appointment. After a battery of tests, you sit in front of the learned doctor and she describes in detail what you need to do to quickly and forever cure your condition. She leaves you with the assurance that if you do these things, your recovery will be complete.

It will be a total waste of time if you don't *do* what the doctor instructs.

Knowing doesn't make you better; *doing* makes you better.

Learning at an intellectual level is both entertaining and enriching, but if your outward life—your interactions with others, the performance of your job, and the impact of your existence—are not positively affected, what good is it?

True learning is a river that flows through us. You gain knowledge and understanding in order to apply it not only for the benefit to yourself but also for those impacted by you and who depend on you. Great learning may start as an abstract concept, but when applied correctly and consistently, it appears as concrete results.

To make your best better, use these ideas to make sure that each day you go to bed smarter than when you woke up.

Actions

1. Become an autodidact.
2. Develop your learning agenda.
3. Periodically review for retention.
4. Apply what you are learning.
5. Ask what new lesson you are using today.

HOW I GET BETTER

Dr. Nido Qubein, President of High Point University

Growing up is always in a continuum.

Every night by bedtime I ask myself a simple question: What did I learn today that I didn't know yesterday? How did I become a better person, leader, parent, friend?

Long ago I committed that I'd invest one-third of my life in earning, one-third in serving, and one-third in learning.

Here's how I get better:

1. Early to bed, early to rise. Out of bed at 4:00 a.m. daily and read/study until 6:00 a.m. Then a brisk one-hour walk to think, ponder, and evaluate.

2. Who you spend time with is who you become. I hang around enough bright, innovative, calculated risk-takers in a variety of venues and sectors. I listen and learn and execute.

3. What you choose is what you get. So I choose to try new things, embark on new initiatives, partner with progressive people. Sometimes I succeed. Sometimes I fail. I celebrate my successes and learn from my failures.

4. Ultimately, getting better demands a commitment, not a decision. You make a decision with your brain. You make a commitment with your heart. Commitments are harder to break and have longer influence.

CHAPTER 6

Deeper Thinking

What You Can Learn from a Famous Sculpture

Thinking is the hardest work there is, which is
probably why so few people engage in it.

—HENRY FORD

The Potential Matrix

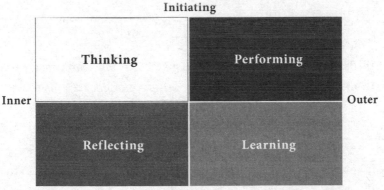

You've seen it, one of the most well-known and recognizable sculptures in the world. You know it as *The Thinker* by Auguste Rodin, but originally it was called *The Poet*. The sculpture was first part of a bigger work called *The Gates of Hell*, based on the works of the poet Dante.

What does *The Thinker* say to you? Most, without pause, would say that thinking is important. While true, there is something more significant to the message of the art.

To understand what I mean, assume the posture of the figure portrayed by *The Thinker*: both feet on the floor, right hand cocked and placed beneath your chin. Then place your right elbow on your left knee. How does it feel? Uncomfortable? Difficult?

Here is how Rodin explained it: "What makes my Thinker think is that he thinks not only with his brain, with his knitted brow, his distended nostrils and compressed lips, but with every muscle of his arms, back, and legs, with his clenched fist and gripping toes."[1]

When was the last time you thought that hard?

WHY THINK?

Thinking is something you do continually but rarely stop to think about—the process is called *metacognition*: thinking about thinking. Intentional and correct thinking offers great benefits.

1. Thinking Creates Your Vision and Your Plans

A vision without thinking becomes a daydream. Thinking is about more than having an idea; it is also about giving form to those ideas and formulating plans. Strategies are ideas with legs.

2. Thinking Enables You to See What Others Don't

The only thing that limits your thinking is your own imagination. People talk about having second thoughts. Effective thinkers have third and fourth thoughts and beyond. Being willing to think better, longer, and harder gives you an edge.

3. Thinking Identifies Important Problems and Solutions

Most problems are easy to identify, tougher to frame, and even harder to solve. You can react to a problem, but finding a solution is proactive. Thinking is about anticipating problems and solving them before they develop or worsen. It is about spotting trends and drawing conclusions about what to do about them.

4. Thinking Eliminates Errors and Assumptions

Inattention to the process of thinking leaves us at risk for unexamined errors and assumptions. Thinking well helps us identify those mistakes and beliefs that potentially keep us from improving.

HOW TO THINK BETTER

We live in an age that seems marked by attention deficit. Our lives have so many competing demands that a modern dilemma seems to be a lack of time to truly think. Yet thinking is the basis for everything that happens. It is risky to allow others to do your thinking for you or to let business and activity minimize the amount of time you devote to conscious thought about your work and life.

Good leaders, managers, parents, and volunteers are always good thinkers. The best—and those who continue to get better—are great thinkers. The following simple suggestions will allow you to undertake better thinking and reap the benefits thinking creates.

1. Make Time to Think

Better thinking takes time, and time is limited. Many days when I'm in Denver, usually midafternoon, I go somewhere to think. I don't take my cell phone. I carry only a pad of paper and a pencil. My objective is to spend fifteen to thirty minutes in uninterrupted thinking.

This proves difficult. Within a few minutes I think of a call I need to return, an e-mail I need to send, or a project I need to work on. Proactive thinking is replaced with responsive thinking.

But thinking is essential. It helps us separate the mundane from the magnificent. It can clarify both our direction and our purposes. It does require that we stop doing business and living life long enough to think about our business and our life.

2. Find a Good Place to Think

Does your home have a "study"? Contemporary homes are more likely to have a "home office," but in the past, men and women would retire to the study after dinner to catch up on work, to plan for the future, and, as the name implies, to study. How much of that activity occurs today is hard to say, but a study can be an excellent place to think, especially if you design it for that purpose. When George Washington was in residence at Mount Vernon, for instance, he spent an average of two hours in the morning and all afternoon alone in his library.[2] But any area that provides calm and a lack of interruption is a good place.

One of my favorite thinking places is about thirty minutes outside of Denver on the side of a small mountain that overlooks the Continental Divide. And I've written two of my books at local coffee shops.

The reason for having a place to think is that a purposeful location quickly enables your thinking mode. When you go to a specific place or spot to do your thinking, the mind becomes conditioned to do just that.

3. Eliminate Errors and Outdated Thinking

Mark Twain is said to have observed, "It ain't what you don't know that gets you into trouble. It's what you know for sure that just ain't so."

To paraphrase Scott Peck, thinking should be the pursuit of reality. To be sound, you should consider questions such as "What do I believe?" and "How do I know this conclusion is true?" and "Says who?" Thinking can be threatening because doing so causes us to reexamine things that we often take for granted.

Moreover, good thinking isn't just about the new things learned but also about the inaccurate things abandoned.

Alvin Toffler is purported to have said, "The illiterate of the 21st century will not be those who cannot read and write but those who cannot learn, unlearn, and relearn."[3]

"Unlearning" is about searching for obsolete thinking. What did you once believe that you no longer believe, or that has been disproved?

Left brain–right brain theory has been popular for years among speakers and consultants, but the latest research finds that it is a highly dubious and less-than-accurate model. Yet it continues to be used because people like it and are comfortable with it.

The truth can set you free, but sometimes it can make you angry. I've found that the truths that often make me the most uncomfortable or that I most resist are often those I most need to accept. Erroneous beliefs seem to have their own natural immunity to the truth, and we tend to guard beliefs that we most want to hold on to, even if they aren't correct.

So, to improve your thinking, you need to be willing to be wrong.

Jack Nicholson said in an interview with *Esquire* magazine, "I love discourse. I'm dying to have my mind changed. I'm probably the only liberal who read *Treason* by Ann Coulter. I want to know, you understand? I like listening to everybody. This to me is the elixir of life."[4] Nicholson is known as one of the greatest actors of our day, but here he revealed himself to be remarkable for a different reason: he is open to new ideas.

Rooting out erroneous or outdated thinking can be hard work, can make us uncomfortable, and may require that we give up ideas we are fond of. But eliminating outdated ideas or thoughts is only a start. We need to go one step further and replace these flawed notions with better ideas and more effective thinking.

Here are some ways to spot errors in thinking:

- Be discerning. Sweeping statements and broad generalities usually aren't true, although there may be some truth in them.
- Understand when something is being oversimplified to save time and effort.
- Look beyond the conventional wisdom. Do your own study before making judgments.
- Identify the exceptions to the rule. Rigidity of thinking causes us to forget that there are often individuals who successfully break the rules. Being aware that there are often, if not always, exceptions to a particular rule keeps us flexible, enables us to challenge the status quo, and prevents us from being surprised and drawing incorrect conclusions when we encounter those exceptions.
- Ask yourself, "What are the irreducible minimums to succeed in this situation or with this project?"

Another error in thinking is "ideacide," the premature killing of an idea before it is considered or tested. Closed thinkers reject out of hand new or unusual ideas. Better thinking requires an openness to fair consideration.

4. Focus Your Thinking

One of the biggest obstacles to thinking is lack of focus. It's true that there can be benefits to letting your mind wander. But this open, spontaneous approach is not always the best one.

To focus your thinking on getting better, start with these five questions:

- Where do I want to improve?
- Why do I want to improve?
- How will I improve?
- When will I start?
- How will I measure success?

5. Write It Down

Over time most people have good ideas. The problem isn't a lack of ideas but a lack of recall. Before you can use an idea, you have to remember it.

Ideas are fleeting and must be captured. Some of the biggest payoffs from thinking will occur when you review notes of previous thinking sessions and add to or modify what you came up with.

Writing down your ideas gives you a chance to review and reevaluate them. Some great ideas I wrote down didn't seem so terrific a couple of weeks later, and some fledgling thoughts have grown, over time, into really good ideas.

6. Stimulate Your Brain

Doug Hall, creativity guru and founder of Eureka! Ranch, believes that coffee is the ultimate thinking elixir (and that's another reason why I sometimes do my thinking at coffee shops). Christopher Marlowe believed good conversation was as stimulating as coffee, and I believe thinking should be as well. But a cup of java to get the process started doesn't hurt.

There are other ways to stimulate your thinking. Reading outside your comfort zone is one. Whether that means choosing a book or magazine that is challenging or simply reading a publication from an unfamiliar field, the point is to introduce new concepts and ideas into your mind. Going over the same familiar road will take you to the same familiar places. Reaching an exotic destination requires a different route.

7. Think About the Four Quadrants of the Potential Matrix

Applying thinking—one of the quadrants of the Potential Matrix—to each of the quadrants can be powerful. Thinking about how you think, as mentioned earlier in the chapter, is called *metacognition*, and while it sounds like heady stuff, it is a fast path to thinking better. In addition to engaging in some metacognition, think about the following:

- your performance and how to improve it
- what you need to learn, want to learn, and the most effective ways for doing that

—

Your homework now, should you choose to accept it, is to schedule time each day to practice the almost-lost art of thinking. For the next five days, put time to think on your calendar and practice the suggestions just discussed. At the end of the period, assess what benefits you've enjoyed.

How smart you are is determined in part by genetics, but

only you determine how well you think. Many people use thinking as a software program running in the background of their brains. Bringing it to the forefront and giving attention to improving it will make you better, not just at thinking itself, but in all the other ways you use it.

Actions

1. Make time to think hard.
2. Focus on thinking about what and how to improve.
3. Eliminate errors and outdated thinking.
4. Stimulate your brain.
5. Write down your thoughts.

HOW I GET BETTER

Randy Pennington, Author and Change Consultant

The definition of *better* changes and increases every day. So for me, the process of getting better begins with the mind-set that you must repeatedly re-earn your value and relevance in the marketplace. It ends with candor, honesty, and accountability about my results. In between, I try to practice the three Ls: look, listen, and learn. I am continuously looking at what the best are doing and comparing that to my own abilities and performance. I listen to what others are saying about what they value, expect from me, and think about my performance. Finally, I work very hard to learn, grow, and adapt in the areas of my work and relationships that are important for my success.

CHAPTER 7

Insightful Introspection

How to Enter the Room with No Door and Accurate Mirrors

All of humanity's problems stem from man's
inability to sit quietly in a room alone.

BLAISE PASCAL, *PENSÉES*

The Potential Matrix

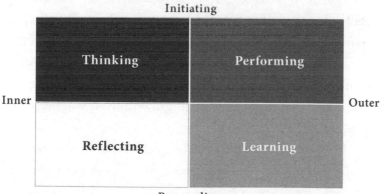

Have you ever had an epiphany? An epiphany is an experience of sudden and striking realization. They are commonly associated with religious experiences and scientific breakthroughs, but they can happen in any situation. When an epiphany occurs, something previously opaque or obscure becomes clear, often to powerful effect.

How often do you have these kinds of powerful insights? Is there a way to have more of them more often? And can they be related specifically to your life—your relationships, your work, and yourself?

Often when we engage in self-reflection, we see distortion, as if we were looking in funhouse mirrors, which create bizarre and sometimes grotesque appearances. We see in a distorted fashion because our perspective is shaped by how others see us, how other cultures compare to ours, how organizations evaluate us, and more. An accurate examination of our emotional and mental processes is difficult. This is not a recent dilemma.

An inscription was carved over the door to the temple of Delphi twenty-four hundred years ago: "Know thyself."

Is it truly possible to know yourself? That has been an abiding question for many deep thinkers. Regardless of your stance on this timeless question, there is a more practical consideration: Even if you may never completely understand yourself, wouldn't there be great gain in knowing yourself better? Might this adage be true: to grow yourself you must first know yourself?

Epiphanies—that is, clarity and deeper understanding about yourself and how to improve your life—happen through introspection.

WHY BE INTROSPECTIVE?

What are the benefits of better understanding yourself?

1. Introspection Helps You See Yourself as You Really Are

A clear view of yourself is essential. It shows the good and the bad, what you are doing right, and where and why you need to improve.

2. Introspection Provides Deeper Understanding

Pascal wrote, "The heart has its reasons which reason knows nothing of." Sometimes there are reasons you can't easily know or understand without contemplation.

Have you ever found yourself doing something for weeks, months, or years, only to one day wonder why? Action without motive is difficult to sustain, and we live in an age when it is easy to be busy and either not know why or have reasons that aren't worthwhile.

3. Introspection Provides Perspective

Introspection contrasts who you are with who you want to be, and what you are doing with what you should be doing. It reveals where you are good enough and where you deeply desire to get better.

4. Introspection Goes Deeper Than Simply Thinking About Things

You can conjure up conscious reasons and explanations through the typical thought process, but contemplation and introspection take you deeper into the less-known areas of your heart and mind.

THE ROOM WITH NO DOOR

When I teach the introspection quadrant, I refer to it as the room with no obvious door. Clients tell me they understand this quadrant in concept but they aren't able to use it well at a practical level.

Think of the times you've read a mystery book or seen a television show where pressing a secret button or moving a book on a shelf suddenly opened a passage to a hidden room. If you didn't know where the button or book was located, you'd never find the room.

Introspection can be that way. We try to reflect deeply and get frustrated by our inability to access the desired space.

In this chapter I'll explain some ways to get into the room of reflection, and then discuss the benefits of what you learn there.

FIVE REASONS
INTROSPECTION IS RARE

1. Lack of Time

How much uninterrupted time do you have each day? Finding time to do the deep work of introspection is probably the biggest challenge and impediment to introspection.

Nicholas Carr, author of *The Shallows*, identified a major impediment to introspection: "Finding moments to engage in contemplative thinking has always been a challenge, since we're distractible, but now that we're carrying these powerful media devices around with us all day long, those opportunities become even less frequent, for the simple reason that we have this ability to distract ourselves constantly."[1]

As a father, I learned that I didn't have time for my kids; I made time. We make time for what we truly value, otherwise we are controlled by schedules imposed by the demands of others.

2. Fear

Denial or avoidance can be the mind's way of protecting us from the unpleasant. I once read an author who said most people weren't too busy to look up from the grindstone; they were afraid to.

Mark Twain purportedly said, "The more I know about people, the better I like my dog." I might amend that statement with my own experience: the more I get to know myself, the more I like my dog. The problem is that an honest evaluation of self can lead to some pretty dismal findings. It can be disappointing. You may be pleased with the genuine good within or mortified with an honest examination of your flaws.

3. Difficulty

Going within is a difficult journey. Introspection is the most difficult of the four quadrants. It is challenging and nebulous, and for many of us, foreign. The other three quadrants for improvement on the potential matrix aren't easy, but this one is the most taxing—and sometimes perplexing.

4. It's a Waste of Time

There are those who focus on the outer world of doing, believing the inner world to be less important or unimportant. I am convinced that the inner world informs the outer world, and that for the majority of us, going within to understand motivations, hopes, fears, and dreams offers some of the greatest leverage to improving every area of our lives.

5. Can't Get There from Here

When the subject of introspection comes up, a guru at the top of the mountain, with folded legs and a distant expression, may come to mind. And there's a reason for that. As much as I've read and studied about introspection and reflection, I've found no clear road map. Although I will offer suggestions, I don't believe in a cookie-cutter approach to such a difficult subject. Instead, experiment. Try the ideas that follow, and adjust to personalize them to your needs.

WHAT INTROSPECTION IS (AND ISN'T)

Introspection Isn't About Slowing Down; It Is About Stopping

The best reflection isn't done "on the fly." You can think while you are in motion—on an exercise bike, walking between meetings, driving to work—but deeper levels of introspection almost always require relaxation, which means lack of movement.

It requires not just rest, but a stilling of the mind.

It is less about what you acquire from the process and more about what you accept.

You think with an outcome in mind. When you introspect, however, the outcome arises as a by-product.

Introspection Isn't Self-Absorption

Isolating from others through introspection either makes you a hermit or a navel gazer. It shouldn't permanently disengage you from the demands of the world and your life. It is a temporary and periodic break that enables you to learn things you wouldn't through thinking and action alone.

Good reflection leads to action, improving both your inner and your outer life.

USING INTROSPECTION BETTER

1. Stop and Make Space to Reflect

It is impossible to be introspective when you are moving at one hundred miles an hour with your hair on fire.

It is important to make time to think. It is also important, and harder, to make space to reflect. Thinking is about using information, while introspection is more about acquiring insight.

You can specifically frame a thinking challenge or a problem: "How do I increase sales?"

In matters of insight from introspection, the process is more general: "How do I feel about my job?" and "Why do I feel that way?"

2. Clear Your Mind of Distractions

Mindfulness is used by many today as a way to clear the mind and focus awareness on the present moment. It teaches the calm acknowledgment and acceptance of your thoughts, feelings, and bodily sensations.

What can distract you in your pursuit of better insights? Worry and anxiety are at the top of the list, as well as frustration at the vagueness of the process. And "demanding" insights that don't always come when you want them.

Clearing the mind is the most difficult aspect of introspection. It isn't something most of us do or experience very often. But it is essential.

3. Narrow Your Attention

Rather than trying to boil the ocean, focus on something significant. You can't effectively focus on too many things. When it comes to reflection, it is better to focus on the most important rather than many secondary considerations.

What areas of reflection can you attend to?

The Emotional

How you feel about your life and work are good guides. Understanding not just what you feel but why you feel that way is eye-opening. Vague feelings don't inform unless you understand them.

The Physical

Is your body trying to tell you something? Aches and pains aren't just inconveniences; they can be guides to what needs attention. I'm not a doctor, but I do believe that deep-seated feelings and experiences directly impact our physical condition.

The Spiritual

What do you believe in matters of faith? If you believe in God, what do you feel he is trying to tell you? In the Old Testament the psalmist wrote, "Wait on the LORD" (Psalm 27:14). What can come out of waiting? Openness to ideas as well as renewed strength is possible.

Prayer is often considered talking with God. In my experience, prayer can be about listening to God and finding that still voice that shares what he wants you to hear.

Meditation and *contemplation* are synonyms, and there are many excellent books and resources on how to meditate, some secular and others religious. I suggest using one or more of them.

4. Quiet the Judge

Eventually you need to discern if something is good, bad, or neutral or if it is helpful or unhelpful. But introspection can be quickly shut down by judgment. As soon as you reach a conclusion, you quit reflecting. If something looks negative or frightening, you don't stay with it.

To keep your heart and mind open, you need to quiet the judge in your head. That judge is essential later in the process as you move between the quadrants of the potential matrix evaluating and then separating better from best—but in the beginning stages of reflection, it can too quickly shut the door to any epiphanies.

———

Each of our lives is a story that can be told and understood in different ways. Introspection allows us to look at our personal narratives so that we can understand not just our individual stories, but also each chapter and sentence. This gives us a chance to improve the stories—yours and mine—not by revising but by reconsidering what has already happened and what it means, and thus writing better sentences and chapters as we move forward.

The point isn't just to understand your story better; the point is to make your story better.

The goal isn't just to *know* more but to *be* more. Epiphanies and insights should lead to adjustments and changes in behavior. They could mean ending some things, realigning others, or taking on new challenges.

You may spend time pondering and not arrive at any huge insights or epiphanies. But whatever thoughts you have could well have value. The challenge is finding ways to apply them to help you better your best.

Actions

1. Fight the fear of reflection.
2. Stop to reflect.
3. Clear your mind.
4. Narrow your attention.
5. Quiet the judge.
6. Hope for, but don't expect, epiphanies.

HOW I GET BETTER

Mark Shupe, Community Life Pastor,
Cherry Hills Community Church

In my counseling studies, I often heard the phrase "Things have to get worse before they will get better." Certainly things not going well can be a catalyst for making changes for the better. But what leads to more effective and lasting change is what I call personal awareness. If I really am going to become a better husband, father, coworker, or person, I first have to take an honest look at the condition of my heart—at my thoughts and motives that lead to my actions. Identifying and owning these sometimes selfish and damaging desires is the first step to becoming a better person. Only by identifying the root issues of my less-than-ideal behavior can I take the steps toward becoming a better person.

PART 3

The Means of Improvement

CHAPTER 8

Disrupt Yourself

If You Don't, Something or Somebody Else Will

To improve is to change; to be
perfect is to change often.

—WINSTON CHURCHILL

Now that you understand *where* you can improve using
the Potential Matrix, you are ready to create breakthrough
improvement by taking four actions: *disrupting yourself, (re)
focusing, engaging others*, and *expanding your capacity*.

John, a college student leader, was making a presentation
to a large audience at a summer camp. The elected leader of
his youth organization, he was an accomplished communicator
and committed performer.

He gave what he considered to be a powerful and successful
presentation. Then the group was dismissed and headed back
to their cabins for the evening.

During the trip back, John caught up with the advisor of his organization. He was a stickler for excellence and had a reputation for being tough but fair.

"So what did you think?" John asked expectantly.

The older, wiser, and respected guide stopped and said simply, "I expected more."

With that, John recalled, "I turned around and headed back to the conference center to get to work." John had been disturbed—you might say, disrupted—by the response, but he decided to do more than be bothered. He chose to disrupt himself and get better for the days ahead.

If you don't disrupt yourself, someone or something else will.

Did you start the day hoping that before it was over you'd be disrupted? You won't find many people who do. Disruption is unsettling at best and unpleasant at worst. It forces change and requires additional effort.

Business literature is filled with articles about, and use of, the word *disruption*. There are disruptive technologies, industries, companies, and sometimes even nations. The disrupters typically are the game changers, often altering things for the better and to their profit. Disruption isn't about change writ small. It is about big, attention-grabbing, smack-you-upside-the-head change. It can be revolutionary, but in all cases one thing is certain: the disrupted are never the same.

Most people and companies wait for disruption to change them. They respond to disruption and call it "change management." In reality, they have no other recourse. They are simply taking the change forced upon them and adapting or even tweaking it for survival. And you can't count on returning to your former level of success once you have been disrupted from the outside.

But what about those committed to getting better? For them, self-disruption is both good and necessary. Self-disrupters unsettle the complacent, challenge mediocrity, drive innovation, and keep people and companies growing. They challenge the status quo, both in themselves and those around them.

What if you and I routinely disrupted ourselves? What if we changed before we had to and innovated when we didn't need to? What would be the benefits?

Here are two crucial differences between other- and self-disruption: Disruption from the outside is imposed and can be necessary for survival. Disruption from within is initiated and necessary for innovation.

Disruption from without changes your game. Disruption from within makes you the game changer.

If you are committed to bettering your best, *disrupt yourself before someone or something else does.*

WHY DISRUPT?

1. Disrupting Yourself Opens the Path to Growth

Not all change is growth, but all growth is change. Unwillingness to confront assumptions, challenge your thinking, and try new things is a roadblock to improvement.

An object in motion is easier to move than an object at rest. Complacency is rest; disruption is motion.

2. Disrupting Yourself Preempts the Competition

Rather than responding, you are creating. Instead of playing catch-up, you are playing stay-ahead. You don't win by playing not to lose.

3. Disrupting Yourself Develops Mental Muscle

Abandon the image of the path to progress as a lovely, level, winding walk in a beautiful countryside. The path to progress is rocky, steep, and challenging. It is a path of resistance, and resistance—like disruption—develops strength.

4. Disrupting Yourself Creates Unforeseen Opportunities

You'll enter territory you've never visited, and if you keep your eyes open, you'll see opportunities either invisible to or unspotted by others.

NEOMANIA ISN'T ALL BAD

Neomania gets a bad rap. It isn't a common word, so it is even less commonly understood. Neomania is the love of the new simply because it is new. Neomaniacs, obsessed and preoccupied with newness, tend to want the latest of anything and everything.

The bad rap comes from the focus on the material and wanting the latest and greatest gadget. And there is a negative connotation around the idea of changing for change's sake, something we are told is a bad thing. But is it always a bad thing?

According to the UK's *Guardian*, nearly 50 percent of us

are "'often bored' at home or at school, while more than two-thirds of us are chronically bored at work." Research suggests a link between this chronic boredom and a variety of negative outcomes, such as "overeating, truancy, antisocial behaviour, drug use, accidents, risk taking and much more."[1]

Neomania is one way to disrupt boredom and spark improvement.

For example, changing the coach on a losing sports team often results in an increase in wins, both for the team the coach left and the new team the coach joins. It may not last, but the change in personnel unsettles the typical and reinvigorates efforts.

Switching things up breaks monotony and routine. The change in itself may or may not be better (and please don't mis-construe this idea by taking foolhardy risks and making costly changes), but breaking up patterns and unsettling stable but humdrum practices can result in new enthusiasm, energy, and opportunities.

LOOK OVER YOUR SHOULDER FOR MOTIVATION

Being an entrepreneur or running a business successfully can be as much about gut-wrenching fear as it is about enthusiasm for your work or pride in your accomplishment. You are only as good as your customer thinks you are. Yesterday's success is no guarantee of tomorrow's success. You know that if you don't keep getting better, you are at risk of being replaced and becoming irrelevant or obsolete.

There are competitors and forces that can be detrimental to your business, and it's crucial that you know how to deal with them. Paranoia is an unreasonable and unhealthy preoccupation with threats, real and imagined. Instead, focus on the real threats that can be anticipated, avoided, or counteracted.

Ask yourself the following questions:

- What two to three changes in the next three to five years will most disrupt the way I've done business?
- Who are my three biggest competitors (individuals, companies, or technologies)
- and why?
- What increased expectations have I seen in my customers?

The more successful you become, the harder it is to stay successful. You stop getting better when you start believing there is no one or no thing that can stop you.

HOW TO DISRUPT YOURSELF

1. Find Who and What Needs Disruption

Ignorance is only temporary bliss to someone who wants to be fully alive and all he or she can be. Denial can be a useful short-term strategy but is often a disastrous long-term strategy.

Disrupting yourself isn't about knowing what needs to be changed; it is about boldly and decisively initiating the change.

You may need to disrupt your habits. First you make habits,

and then one day your habits start to make you. Eliminating a habit doesn't often work, unless you replace it with a healthier, better habit.

Consider what practices need to be disrupted in your life. You may be doing things that used to succeed even though they no longer work as well—or function at all.

Think about disrupting your routines. I used to read two newspapers each day before work. It was enjoyable and partially informative. There was much overlap in each paper, and I'd heard the headlines previously on CNN while working out. So, I stopped reading two newspapers as a routine. It saved thirty to sixty minutes of time and gave me the chance to jump-start my day with more productive activities.

A dream that you're not actively trying to achieve is a daydream. Disrupt it. I am a licensed pilot, but I haven't been current for many years. I have often thought, and dreamed, of updating my skills, getting current, and flying again. After several years of thinking about it, and even searching out some good flight instruction, I realized that with the other priorities in my life, it wasn't going to happen. I let it go. That doesn't mean I won't ever fly again. But disrupting my daydream freed up energy and attention that could be better used.

The hardest disruptions can be relational. If there are people who are negative or unhealthy influences, you may need to change, limit, or end your relationship with them. If you are a manager, there may be someone on your team who needs to be disrupted: either the employee becomes effective at his or her job or that individual finds a better employment fit elsewhere.

2. Ask Disruptive Questions

"We live in the world our questions create."

—David Cooperrider

Knowing the right answers doesn't count if you're asking the wrong questions. It may be good to know much, but it is better to know the important things that will help you get better. Here are some questions to ask yourself.

- What is the most important lesson I have learned this past year?
- What am I doing out of habit that doesn't serve me well?
- What one change in my lifestyle would most improve my health?
- Who should I be spending more time with?
- What could be improved by using new technology?
- When did I not listen to my intuition and later regret it?
- What do I miss doing that I once enjoyed?
- What would I most like to learn?
- What do I most need to learn?
- What is the most important thing I should stop doing?
- What is the most important thing I should start doing?
- What three things would I most like to accomplish in the year ahead?
- What is my biggest time waster?
- Am I aiming too low or aiming too high?
- What is my worst fault? At work? At home?

These questions aren't meant to focus you on the negative, but to get your brain's attention so you can address changes that, once made, create dramatic improvement.

3. Use Your Mistakes to Disruptive Advantage

"A man's errors are his portals of discovery."

—JAMES JOYCE

Mistakes can slow your efforts at improvement and demoralize you. But there are two kinds of mistakes: those that set you back and those that educate you.

To be clear, there is no smart way to make a stupid mistake. A stupid mistake or even a dumb decision is either caused by carelessness (antidote: be more careful) or because you know better but still choose to act badly. If you know in advance you're doing something really stupid, the only option is not to do it. (The famous last words before a stupid mistake or decision? "Hey, guys, watch this!")

How can your mistakes help you get better?

First, admit the mistake. You can't learn as much from a mistake you don't own. Denial only makes the mistake you made worse. Second, accept responsibility. Many are quick to take credit but even quicker to place blame. Don't pass the buck (which as a side benefit will raise your credibility in the eyes of most rational people).

Third, fix what you can. There may be some things you can do to mitigate the mistake, lessen any damage, take corrective action, or make apologies or even amends if your mistake negatively affects others. If there is something you can do to lessen the cost, do it quickly.

Fourth, learn what you can. Experience is a good teacher only if you're paying attention and learning from it. Ask others what you can learn from your mistake. Leverage your lessons or insights by sharing your mistake with others who might make similar errors.

4. Disrupt Yourself with Old Ideas

C. S. Lewis, the British author and Christian apologist, was also professor of medieval and Renaissance literature at Magdalene College, Cambridge. He had a love for the ideas from those eras because of their beauty and timelessness. And he charged those who didn't value those ideas or eras with what he termed "chronological snobbery."[2] Chronological snobs believe that the thinking, art, or science of an earlier time is inherently inferior when compared to that of the present. As a result, they dismiss the old regardless of its potential relevance and usefulness.

Because old ideas are often overlooked or forgotten, they can be rich resources of disruption. Being unfamiliar and unused by most, these old ideas can bring new disruption: using the past to disrupt the present, if you will. Although our culture has changed, many of the concepts discussed and debated long ago are timeless. You need only to find new ways to apply the wisdom, and in doing so, you will disrupt the modern and accepted with the ancient and ignored.

BE BRAVE

Self-disruption will require you to be brave. I don't mean to sound melodramatic, but self-disruption is not for the faint of heart.

Being creatures of habit, many of us are deficient in the flexibility department. We like to stick to the plan, do things the way we've always done them, and put as many things on autopilot as possible. We lull ourselves into a routine that closes us off to the flexibility required for self-disruption.

Self-disruption can be risky. It is about abandoning certainty. Even when you stop doing what didn't work, there are no guarantees for what will work.

Do it anyway.

Actions

1. Identify who or what needs to be disrupted in your life.
2. Switch things up to keep your journey interesting.
3. Ask more disruptive questions.
4. Pull the lessons from your mistakes and failures.
5. Disrupt yourself with old ideas.

HOW I GET BETTER

Scott McKain, Author, Professional Speaker, Consultant

A business crisis is a great motivator to reinvent. Several years ago, my revenue was down, momentum was nonexistent, and I was left with a mountain of bills. I started asking speakers bureaus—similar in professional speaking to manufacturers' representatives in other industries—what they were saying when they recommended my services to their clients. The top answer: "Nice guy. Good speaker." I was horrified! I choose to be nice, and I want to be a good speaker, but prospects weren't seeking that combination. Potential clients desire an author or speaker who can deliver top-notch content in a compelling manner. I chose to refocus and reinvent. I studied the elements of creating distinction in my marketplace—and discovered it was a topic that prospective clients were also very interested in learning. This refocusing has created the professional success I now enjoy.

CHAPTER 9

(re)Focus

The Antidote to Perpetual Distraction

What preoccupies the mind controls the life.

—Timothy Keller

A friend was searching for his cell phone and explained this to the person he was talking to—on his cell phone.

We live in the age of perpetual distraction and the antidote to this is focus.

But being alert isn't helpful if you aren't focused on the right things.

How focused are you right now? Are you reading these words while scanning your smartphone for a text and simultaneously checking for new e-mails? Are you fully present in the moment or wondering what's for dinner tonight?

There are so many different things that can distract us personally as well as professionally. The digital age has fully enveloped our minds, evidenced by the fact that people communicate more through e-mails, text messages, and social networking than they do face-to-face or even over the telephone.

The average person at work checks his or her e-mail thirty times an hour. While acknowledging that e-mail can be important, can you imagine all of the things that you could accomplish in your day if you stayed consistently focused on other and more important things?

On the path toward achieving long-term success professionally, you'll encounter obstacles and detours. You can't control all of them, but you can control your focus.

Distraction impedes getting better. The solution? (re)Focus.

WHY (RE)FOCUS?

1. (re)Focusing Saves Time and Energy

You'll stop wasting time on low-priority or ineffective activities and spend more time on those things that will produce your greatest results and improvement.

2. (re)Focusing Keeps You (or Puts You Back) on Track

We all get off track periodically and need to readjust. (re)Focusing isn't just about doing new and different things, but rather is about bringing your efforts into alignment with current needs and realities.

3. (re)Focusing Brings Others into Alignment

If you're a leader, your team takes its cues from you. When you're focused, you send a strong message about what you need to be doing.

4. (re)Focusing Speeds Results

You can't get great results doing the wrong things quickly. (re) Focusing is an appraisal of what will get you the best results fastest.

HOW TO (RE)FOCUS

1. Challenge Your Current Focus

> "I just want people to take a step back, take a deep breath and actually look at something with a different perspective. But most people will never do that."
>
> —BRIAN McKNIGHT

Success can be an early-warning indicator for failure. As my pal Joe Calloway says, "Success only means you know what worked yesterday."

Doing the same things out of unexamined habit is dangerous. You'll get better by replacing the wrong or low-payoff activities with more productive behaviors. That means you need to regularly reevaluate.

What did I do in the past that I should start doing again? Sometimes we don't exactly abandon good practices; they just slip away. Over time we either do them less, not as well, or not at all because we get busy and forget. What one thing, if you started doing it again, would bring you the most results? In other words, what used to work, and will still work, if you consistently did it?

What should I stop doing?

Just because something used to work doesn't mean it will always succeed. But you'd never know it from the obsession some people and organizations have with replicating the past even when it isn't creating the results they desire. Elimination of outdated or less-effective processes and practices should be your first task.

What should I start doing?

New skills and behaviors usually require a learning curve, so we tend to put off doing them. Get rigorous in identifying what you need to do, and start developing that ability. The things you stop doing need to be replaced with things that will make you more effective, efficient, and better.

What should I do differently?

Modifying a practice or process to make it better is always a priority.

One financial planner I know realized that he had access to the same investment information as everyone else. While he was great at explaining to clients how to take advantage of the information, he realized he could get better by finding new ideas sooner and getting the information to his clients faster. Compared to the competition, he developed a competitive advantage based on speed.

2. Stop Multitasking

One of the biggest barriers to getting better is multitasking.

Many people frequently brag about being good at multitasking. Well, it appears that they are going in the wrong direction. Recent research has concluded that it takes those people longer to do their work; plus, they won't do it as well.[1]

We think of multitasking as the ability to successfully perform more than one activity at the same time. It has become a seemingly ubiquitous phenomenon, like walking in the park while talking to a friend. But there is a difference: walking doesn't require your cognitive attention, so you are free to concentrate on your conversation. Other situations, such as trying to read a book while listening to a lecture, are more complex.

In reality, what is commonly referred to as multitasking is the rapid shifting of attention from one task to another. That is what creates the illusion that you are performing them concurrently.

Nancy K. Napier, PhD, in her article "The Myth of Multitasking," wrote, "Much recent neuroscience research tells us that the brain doesn't do tasks simultaneously, as we thought (hoped) it might. In fact, we just switch tasks quickly. Each time we move from hearing music to writing a text or talking to someone, there is a stop/start process that goes on in the brain."[2] This rapid switching of tasks is tedious, makes us prone to error and loss of concentration, and ends up consuming more time than if we undertook one task at a time.

And all the switching comes at a neurobiological cost. There is a structure in the brain responsible for switching tasks. Every time we change tasks, the brain responds by triggering a neurochemical switch that involves the consumption of glucose, which is limited in supply. After a series of rapid switch activities, so much glucose is depleted we tend to feel worn-out. This diminishes essential neural resources, inhibits right thinking, and leads to errors.

Another problem is attention residue. Sophie Leroy, a professor at the University of Minnesota, found that it is difficult for people to switch their full attention to a new task. There is carryover from the previous unfinished one that prevents giving the new work complete focus, and that explains the term *attention residue*.[3]

Workplace demands often create the perceived need to continually switch tasks. Unfortunately, that makes people less efficient. When you suspend one task to undertake another, you end up carrying baggage from your previous work into the next undertaking, and the desired results are diminished.

In short, it is more productive, more fulfilling, and less time-consuming to concentrate on one task and, if possible, to complete it before undertaking a new one.

The ability to do a thing well and quickly requires full attention, and the myth of multitasking prevents that from occurring. Improvement in any area is a function of the capacity to pay attention. Isaac Newton, for example, credited his many successes and discoveries as "owing more to patient attention than to any other talent."

Stop fooling yourself. You're not truly multitasking; in reality, you're task switching. And that's fine if that's what you want to do. But there is a better way.

3. Block Uninterrupted Time to Work on Important Improvements

(re)Focus on being better at the beginning of each day. Start by identifying the most significant work, tasks, and projects that you need to accomplish. Schedule a specific time to work on them, rather than attempting them between other tasks.

Aim for at least thirty to sixty minutes without phone calls, walk-ins, or other distractions. Choose to focus your attention on one thing at a time.

(re)Focus means you know what is important, and you recognize that you can be easily distracted and diverted if you don't commit time to concentrating on doing the work.

4. Make (re)Focus an Ongoing Process

We need to constantly check the things we're focused on to make sure they are the best and highest-priority items on our agenda. As the speed of change increases, so, too, does our need to (re)focus. What made sense last week might not make nearly as much sense this week. Clients, colleagues, our employers—they all change their focus, and that has an impact on us. It isn't enough to be focused if you aren't in sync with the changing focus of those who depend on you.

DEEPER THINKING

(re)Focusing is how you turn your thinking, goals, plans, and vision into reality. Create an agenda after deep thinking. Identify what you will do, who you will involve, the resources you'll need, and a timeline. This will keep you focused and put the next steps top of mind.

INSIGHTFUL INTROSPECTION

True epiphanies and deep insights are typically less plentiful than good ideas gained from thinking. I've found they are often overarching themes for life. What if you set a goal to focus on one deep insight weekly? At the top of your calendar or planning tool, write down the deepest insight you've gleaned, and then translate that into actions large and small each day.

As I was writing this, I read an article about research on how to lose belly fat. As I thought about it later, what most impressed me was that of the four groups of participants in that study, the most successful were those who simply reduced portion size. They ate all the same things they normally ate, but still lost weight. So, I have made portion control part of my daily focus.

ESCALATING PERFORMANCE

You won't improve your performance if you don't pay attention and note the lessons of practice and application.

Note what does or doesn't work and what could work better. Enter those findings into the way you codify (or summarize and remember) your performance, which I referenced earlier. Evaluation can create useful self-feedback to feed a virtuous loop of escalating performance.

ADVANCED LEARNING

Megachurch pastor Rick Warren talks about listening to sermons as a child and in his notes continually writing *YBH*: "Yes, but how?"[4]

Learning is more than knowing what to do. You also need to understand why you should do it (that provides motivation) and how (that is the technique of application).

You learn best what you implement most quickly. Try to leave a class or meeting with a mentor with one or two key things to try, and the sooner, the better.

(RE)FOCUS IS ABOUT ACCOMPLISHMENT, NOT ACTIVITY

Your improvement is about getting better, not getting tired. Being tired at the end of the day means you were busy, but it doesn't mean you were productive or improving. Working with intensity on a few things is better than being busy with many things.

To get better don't dabble. Instead, drill down.

Dabbling is a trickle of attention and effort. Dabblers start with enthusiasm, but once they achieve the quick and easy gains of improvement, they stop far short of getting the full benefit. Drilling down combines focus and intensity with high-priority and high-return tasks.

Getting better is about increased accomplishment, and while that might take additional effort and activity, being too busy is a sign you aren't being efficient at your improvement.

At the end of the day, ask yourself what you accomplished, not just how busy you were. Sometimes we get better by doing less of the things that are low priority or yield minimal results.

Actions

1. Challenge assumptions (quit doing what doesn't serve you best).
2. Stop multitasking.
3. Block times to concentrate on what is most important.
4. (re)Focus based on the quadrants of the Potential Matrix.

HOW I GET BETTER

Larry Winget, TV Personality

I was a successful motivational speaker and got sick of saying things I no longer fully believed just because I was good at saying them and because they sold well. I completely changed my message, appearance, and reputation to become The World's Only Irritational Speaker® and The Pitbull of Personal Development®. That move to become authentic in order to say what I believed at my deepest core was the best thing I ever did, not only personally, but professionally. To become better, sometimes you have to turn things upside down. It takes guts, confidence, and the willingness to become uncomfortable, but the payoff can be huge.

CHAPTER 10

Engage Others

The Keys to Uncommon Improvement

"I'm a self-made man, but if I had to do it over, I'd call in someone else." That was inscribed on a humorous sign that my father, Les Sanborn, kept on display. It's funny, but it raises a question: Are successful people self-made?

There's an old saying that if you see a turtle on top of a fence post, you can be sure he didn't get there by himself. I don't know of many successful people who aren't like the turtle. They've taken responsibility and done the work, but others have provided ideas, mentoring, coaching, encouragement, and more. Avail yourself of the wisdom and help of others, and you'll go further faster.

Self-responsibility is the primary step toward a successful life. But engaging others and building mutually beneficial relationships will leverage everything you do.

UNCOMMON FRIENDS

Jim Newton was a real-estate developer in Fort Myers, Florida, in the early 1900s. What made him unique was his friendship with five historic figures.

Who were these uncommon friends?

- **Thomas Edison:** inventor extraordinaire. His inventions, which greatly influenced life all over the world, include the phonograph, the motion picture camera, and the electric lightbulb.
- **Henry Ford:** industrialist, founder of the Ford Motor Company, and pioneer of the modern assembly line.
- **Charles Lindbergh:** aviation hero who piloted the *Spirit of St. Louis* on the first transatlantic solo flight. He was also an explorer and inventor.
- **Harvey Firestone:** the founder of Firestone Tire and Rubber Company and one of the first global manufacturers of automobile tires.
- **Alexis Carrel:** French surgeon and biologist who pioneered vascular suturing techniques.

Newton reported in his book *Uncommon Friends* (Thomson Learning, 1989) that these titans of business and industry shared similar interests and philosophies.

Not only did Jim Newton and these five business leaders live near one another and fish, dine, and socialize together;

they learned and improved as a group. Each man's individual perspectives and ideas challenged, sharpened, and expanded the others' thinking.

Think of having regular conversations with the technology, business, and political leaders of our day. Consider the amazing things you could learn not just from reading and listening but also from engaging, asking questions, and discussing interests. We become greater by association, not just by being around other great people, but also by connecting with them.

Marie Arana-Ward, the editor of *Uncommon Friends*, said, "Friendship can be a springboard to greatness and creativity; in cultivating their friends, each of the uncommon friends became a broader human being with more to contribute to their country's culture."[1]

Not every person who is a resource to your improvement will become a close, personal friend (obviously, most won't). Still, *Uncommon Friends* points to the power of engaging others at many levels to enrich and improve your life.

As you think about ways to deepen engagement to improve, remember: others can help you get better, but they can't make you get better. Their concern, aid, support, and encouragement can only benefit you when you are willing to do what is necessary to better your best.

"Don't burn bridges" is good advice. Better advice is to "maintain bridges."

Knowing what to ask is important. Knowing who to ask is critical.

WHY ENGAGE OTHERS?

1. Engaging Others Deepens Relationships

It is a blessing to improve and an even greater blessing to engage others in deeper, more meaningful relationships through learning and sharing ideas.

2. Engaging Others Creates Networks

A successful organization, of any size, is a network of talented and like-minded individuals. Those you engage personally become part of your extended network.

3. Engaging Others Leverages Improvement

Nobody has enough time to learn everything on his or her own. I joined a professional association more than thirty years ago because I knew it would cut years off my learning curve. And it did.

4. Engaging Others Saves Time

You can acquire knowledge from the success and failure of others. That will help you replicate their victories and hopefully avoid some of the things that lead to failure.

FIRST THINK *WHAT,* THEN *WHO*

According to Anders Ericsson, author of *Peak: Secrets from the New Science of Expertise,* "The most optimal way to improve your performance is to find a teacher who has been teaching other people to reach the level of performance that you want to attain."[2]

Many of the people around us possess wisdom, but we don't benefit completely from it by simply observing. We have to engage people deeply in order to access the wisdom they have to offer.

Some friends help us improve and some hinder us. Not everyone is as committed to improvement as you are, and while this is fine for them, it can be a detriment for you.

I've found that a shared commitment to improvement and success can be (and maybe should be) an ingredient to a rewarding friendship. In my life, the Five Friends started as a group of individuals whose friendship spans more than years. Over time, as we shared ideas and learned from one another, we decided to formalize the relationship and create a brand that today collaborates on writing, video production, coaching, and events.

ENGAGE IN A DIVERSITY OF WAYS

Joining a study group or professional association is a great path to improvement. The education and community those kinds of organizations offer give you both the ideas and the support to improve.

Another path is by formally engaging an individual who can advise, coach, or mentor you on a regular basis. The process for doing this will need to be agreed upon by both of you.

Yet another way is by doing something I've practiced for some time now: I periodically hold sessions in my office where

I invite three to four people with interesting ideas and perspectives to meet for two hours to discuss a topic.

The best ways to learn from others include both depth and diversity.

SOME RULES OF ENGAGEMENT

1. To Become the Best, Engage the Best

Emulation is one of the quickest ways to learn. Do you know who the best people are in your field or area of interest? Are you familiar with the top performers? Who do you look to as an example to learn from?

Don't just study what the best do; make sure you learn how they think. Doing something without understanding why is foolish. By knowing how the best think, you'll be able to assess what you should be doing.

2. Ask Yourself Two Questions

First, how would the best do this?

When you've committed to a course of action, analyze how the best implement and execute. Study the process peak performers use to achieve results.

Want to be a better speaker? Study the best, and pay as much attention to how they say something as to what they say. If you need to move people to action, study the finest inspirational or motivational speakers and learn how their choice of words, use of stories, variance in volume, speed of delivery, and other behaviors contribute to their success.

Second, how might I do it even better?

Nobody has a corner on perfection. Just as the best performers continue to get better, you can learn what is working now and look for ways to polish, adjust, and improve. Don't stay stuck in the past. Challenge yourself by seeing how you can improve on best practices and make them even better.

3. Consider the Sources

Ralph Waldo Emerson loved to ask the people he encountered, "What has become clear to you since we last met?" He wanted to extract the counsel and best thinking of others.

What is good advice? It is information relevant to you and your business based on where you are at a particular point in time. Advice that comes too late or too early won't be helpful to you. And you must be receptive to what it suggests you do.

But remember what my friend Larry Winget says: Be careful who you take advice from. Listen to people who have actually done something, not just people who talk about its having been done (usually by someone else).

4. Be a Qualified Recipient

To best benefit from the counsel of others, you need to meet three conditions:

Find a way to relate the counsel to your
work, projects, and/or improvement.

The relevancy of the advice is dependent on the person and their situation.

Make sure the timing is right for you.

Sometimes advice arrives when you're not in a position to apply it immediately. There are more urgent or pressing matters to attend to, or you don't have the necessary resources. If this is the case, put it on your "to do as soon as possible" list.

Sometimes it is the "wrong time" because that advice might be too uncomfortable or painful. You need to wait until you're able to accept it gracefully.

Be willing to consider suggestions and
advice even when it's difficult.

You might not like the advice you're getting because it is hard or painful to accept. Remember that the best advice often comes from friends and colleagues who love you enough to tell you the truth. Don't let the unpleasantness of advice prevent you from recognizing its value.

5. Consider Forming a Mastermind Group

A *mastermind group* is a group of highly motivated individuals committed to helping one another improve a specific area or areas of their lives.

Over thirty years I've belonged to several successful and supportive mastermind groups. As a result, I've been asked to speak and consult on how to form an effective mastermind group. It is a large topic, but the most important steps are these:

First, identify the specific reason for inviting like-minded and interested people to join the mastermind group. Participation depends on everyone's being clear about why the group exists.

Next, agree on the benefits members want to gain. Clarity is the first value, and motivation is the second.

Finally, discuss how each member can participate. Make it easy for people to be valuable contributors by talking about expectations.

The most important thing I've learned about mastermind groups is this: They must be mutually beneficial. If they are not, a member—or members—will quit because of perceived disequilibrium. Inevitably, someone will feel that he or she is giving more than he or she is receiving.

Once you've established the higher purpose of the group, you'll need to address these logistical questions:

- How often do we meet?
- What will we do when we meet?
- What will happen in the interim (monthly reports, conference calls, personal meetings)?
- What will it cost in time, money, and energy?

6. Return the Favor

My many friends who are speakers, consultants, and experts in various fields report a similar experience. They are asked for fifteen minutes of their time, or a lunch or conversation over coffee, so someone—often a stranger—can pick their brains.

Beyond the demands on their time, the most disheartening thing that happens after these engagements is . . . nothing. They receive no note of appreciation or follow-up of action taken. That makes them (and I have had similar experiences) feel as though the time was wasted. That's why I suggest you always "pay for free advice." If you engage someone not well-known to you, explain why you are making the request and what you are willing to do if the adviser agrees. That would at least include paying for the meal and following up via e-mail with what you've done with the individual's suggestions, making a donation to his or her favorite charity, or offering to reimburse the expert for his or her expertise.

But perhaps the best way to return the favor is to pass it on. Become a resource to others, and share as willingly as you've had others share with you.

Anything you ever wanted to know or learn has probably already been mastered by someone in history. As noted earlier, today you can access that knowledge easily on the Internet, and that same technology can enable you to engage, listen to, interact with, and learn from others. But keep in mind that while it is relatively easy to access information, doing so while building and maintaining relationships is an even more powerful weapon in your getting-better arsenal. All you have to do is engage deeper.

Actions

1. Start with who knows best.
2. Solicit advice, ideas, and counsel.
3. Engage more deeply and in a variety of ways.
4. Form a mastermind group.
5. Always pay for free advice.

HOW I GET BETTER

Marty Grunder, Owner, Grunder Landscaping

Getting better is a mind-set; you have to want to get better. I get better by asking for help. As an entrepreneur, I learned that early, and thirty-four years later, as the owner of a successful small business, I still ask for help. My team, my clients, my advisors, my banker, my accountant, our vendors, even outgoing team members are all asked to tell us what we could do better. At first I was uncomfortable asking for help. I perceived it to be a sign of weakness. Today I have a passion to get better. I search for ways to delight clients, save time, improve profitability, reduce turnover, and improve my business, my family, my health, my life. The only way in my mind you get better is if you let everyone know you want help and need help. You will be amazed at how many come forward to assist you.

CHAPTER 11

Increasing Capacity

The Secret of the Partially Filled Glass

The remarkable thing is that it is the crowded
life that is most easily remembered. A life
full of turns, achievements, disappointments,
surprises, and crisis is a life full of landmarks.
The empty life has even its few details blurred
and cannot be remembered with certainty.

—ERIC HOFFER

Is the cup half-empty or half-full?

The perpetual question, asked to determine if someone is an optimist or a pessimist, can be answered a number of ways, some humorous. For instance, an engineer replies, "Neither. You simply have twice as much glass as you need."

But there is a better way to answer the question than "full," "empty," or with humor. The way I see it, the answer is simply, "There is room for more."

The glass has something in it, but there is still space. You would be hard-pressed to identify your life as half, two-thirds, or completely full in any of the four areas of the Potential Matrix. And while I don't know you, I claim with certainty: there is room for more.

Andrew Shapiro is proof of that.

Inspired by his father's triumphant five-year battle with cancer, Andrew, a junior in high school, committed himself to setting a Guinness World Record doing pull-ups. He practiced incessantly with the goal of setting three world records during a Relay for Life event in Fairfax County, Virginia.

Early on a Saturday, he began his pull-up marathon. Within six hours, he'd completed 3,515 pull-ups—a new world record. By twelve hours, he had finished 5,742 pull-ups—another world record. Then he set his sights on a final record—the most pull-ups performed in twenty-four hours: 6,800 completed by Czech Republic athlete Jan Kares in 2015.

At the fifteen-hour mark, Shapiro matched Kares's twenty-four-hour record and kept going.

After eighteen hours, Shapiro stopped, having completed 7,306 pull-ups. (In the process, he raised $4,000 for the American Cancer Society.)

Those three records were the culmination of extensive and intensive training. For endurance, Andrew performed 10 pull-ups a minute for six hours. To pass the time, he watched movies.

"It was blood, sweat and hours and hours and hours of hard work," he recounts. He became friends with aching muscles and blistered hands.[1]

Increasing capabilities to Andrew Shapiro's level of skill can be summarized by this equation:

$$time \times effort = capacity$$

Let me remind you of something I said earlier: *you can get better at anything, but you can't get better at everything, at least not significantly.* Why? There just isn't enough time. To become world-class at anything is extremely demanding. For instance, Andrew gave up baseball for an entire season to devote himself to training full-time to set the pull-up record.

What are you willing to exchange for getting better? Resources you spend getting dramatically better in one area can't be devoted to other areas.

WHY INCREASE CAPACITY?

1. Increasing Capacity Provides More Tools for Your Life Kit

Although Ross Ashby pioneered the law of requisite variety in the context of regulation in biology and how organisms adapt, there is a practical use that says the more items you possess in your repertoire of life skills, the more you can successfully deal with the range and variety of challenges you face.

2. Increasing Capacity Fulfills More of Your Potential and Actual Output

Being able to do anything well and quickly increases output and frees up time for developing additional skills.

3. Increasing Capacity Supports and Leverages Other Development

When you know how and what you're trying to improve, you can develop or further develop skills that will complement one another toward that end (more on that in a moment).

4. Increasing Capacity Is Bolstered by Confidence Built in Layers

Whether or not you believe you can do something determines whether or not you try. As you are about to learn, confidence isn't something you either have or don't have. Rather, it can be developed in stages and in varieties that can increase your willingness to attempt new things.

HOW TO INCREASE YOUR CAPACITY AND CONFIDENCE

1. Inventory What You Already Have

What are you already good at? You get better by both *exploiting* what you already know and the skills you've developed and by *exploring* new skills and knowledge.

In the movie *Bridge of Spies*, Mark Rylance plays the Russian spy Rudolf Abel. He is unruffled even when he is captured and facing dire consequences. At several times during the movie, Abel is asked why he doesn't worry or get upset. His response: "Will it help?"

To increase capacity, you need to ask the same question

about the things you do each day. What are the skills you want to develop and the lessons you want to learn? What do you think you need to do? You need to ask: "Will it help?"

What one or two skills, if more fully developed and consistently deployed, would make the biggest difference in your personal and professional improvement?

What one thing, if you started doing it and kept doing it, would give you the biggest return on your investment of time and energy?

2. Add Complementary Skills

According to John H. Zenger, Joseph Folkman, and Scott Edinger, writing in the *Harvard Business Review*, adding complementary strengths to your skills package significantly compounds success.

"Forget about your weaknesses and move on," Zenger says. "In our research of more than 250,000 leaders, we've found specific competencies that produce positive results. Leaders who are strong in certain competencies will achieve the most when they forget about correcting their weakness and focus instead on further enhancing their strengths."[2]

I agree that there is little to be gained from focusing on fixing weaknesses first unless that particular weakness is debilitating to achieving your goals.

Make sure you know which new skills, if developed, will enhance your existing skills toward the improvement in performance you desire. And study what the most important skills are in your priority areas. (Zenger and his colleagues, for instance, studied leaders and leadership skills.)

3. Track Progress or Regress

Vague objectives create vague results. It is often hard to quantify the improvement you desire and just as hard or harder to measure it. Picking a specific capacity to expand is more effective than trying to randomly get better.

To determine how to track progress, start with a simple question: How will I know I am getting better? Feelings aren't an accurate indicator. They can indicate both real and false confidence.

One way to measure expanded capacity is to compare new output against past output. That means maintaining the same level of effort. (Working twice as hard will probably increase output but is no proof of expanded capacity.)

Sometimes you will get worse before you get better. Literally. Adding new skills and trying different things can throw you off balance. It takes time to settle back into a groove and benefit from the additions.

4. Practice as Much as You Can

Did your boss ask you to start this workday spending some time practicing your job? (I'm guessing the answer is no.)

Did you make time this morning to practice the skills upon which your livelihood (and your potential encores) depend, between getting the kids off to school, battling traffic, and riffling through the pile of papers on your desk? (Again, I'm guessing no.)

Let's face it: "practice" conjures up images of artists, athletes, and actors—not people in the workaday world. So, where does that leave the rest of us? Very few people in the world of work practice. The closest they come is a kind of "practice in process"—hoping that the more they do their jobs, the better they'll get. And if they're lucky, practice in process does help more than it hurts.

But if you're going to become a remarkable performer, you're going to have to learn a different way to practice. Instead of just repeating a process, you need to learn to rehearse prior to performing.

Ask any artist, athlete, or actor: Practice is the key to remarkable performance. Without it, your performing days—not to mention your encores—may be numbered.

"Miss one day of practice, I notice; miss two, the critics notice; miss three, the audience notices." While musicians from Liszt to von Bulow to Rubinstein have been said to have made that statement, it is most commonly believed to have been said by Ignacy Jan Paderewski in 1911.

Remember the concept of deliberate practice?

If you think that term suggests that I'm talking about something beyond normal practice, you're right. Researcher and senior editor at *Fortune* magazine Geoffrey Colvin differentiates between practice and deliberate practice this way: "Simply hitting a bucket of balls is not deliberate practice, which is why most golfers don't get better. Hitting an eight-iron 300 times with a goal of leaving the ball within 20 feet of the pin 80 percent of the time, continually observing results and making appropriate adjustments, and doing that for hours every day—that's deliberate practice."[3]

Deliberate practice builds on what you already know and use, that is, repetition (practicing the right way) with feedback from others. Feedback is critical. Whenever possible, ask for feedback from knowledgeable people who observe your performance or work. The person can be a manager, client, coworker, teammate, or someone else who will give you an honest assessment.

Given that example, it's not hard to figure out why the crowd is small at the top of any given mountain. Deliberate practice means daily incorporating new insights and understanding. In other words, deliberate practice requires learning and building on the fruits of that learning.

5. Expand Your Experience

The Center for Creative Leadership (CCL) has studied how to best develop leadership abilities, and they've found that many companies get it backward.

Most companies provide books and training and might provide a mentorship program, but they rarely structure real-world leadership experiences for up-and-coming leaders.

CCL found that the mix should be 70 percent experiences, 20 percent mentors, and 10 percent books.[4]

This certainly is true in my work with helping individuals improve.

Doing the same things repeatedly will help you master those things, but it won't give you a bigger repertoire for your improvement. In addition to aiming at key skills, you can expand your experience by

- trying old things in a new way
- trying new things
- doing the opposite of what you've done

- changing job roles temporarily
- volunteering at a nonprofit
- chairing a project at your house of worship

6. Layer Your Confidence

Capacity is your ability to produce. Confidence is your belief about your capacity.

Success breeds confidence, and confidence breeds success. But confidence doesn't come naturally for most of us. Unfortunately, we think we either do or don't have it. In my observation, confidence is more nuanced and can be developed in layers. Here's how:

Start at the bottom and work up.

Level 1: the confidence to try. The goal at this level is attempting the discipline, not success. If you only do the things you are great at, you won't do much in life. You seldom start at the top. You have to foster an understanding of what it feels like to give something new a try.

Level 2: the confidence to learn. Here the goal is growth. You've tried it and you've gotten some instruction and feedback, so now you feel the confidence to grow and improve.

Level 3: the confidence to do. You've learned enough to feel competent living out what you've learned on a consistent basis. You believe in yourself and your skills.

Level 4: the confidence to master. Here you live it well, and consistently, enough that you can teach it to others. You replicate or reproduce your skills—and your confidence.

7. Get Granular

Look for nuances for improvement, the little things that make a noticeable or pronounced difference.

The better you get, the more challenging it is to get better. When you are good at doing the big things, only by paying extra attention to the little things can you improve your performance. That is the power of nuance.

One of my favorite advisors in professional speaking was a man named Ron Arden. Ron started his career in theater and then spent the latter years of his life coaching very successful speakers.

Ron was the master of nuance. I once worked with him for a day on my own speaking skills. Back then he had asked for a video of one of my presentations. I sent him an hour-long program thinking we'd work through it in the eight hours we had together.

We made it to the eighth minute of my presentation. I learned about the power of a pause and how to use it for greater impact, the nuances of beginning a speech effectively, several bad habits to eliminate, and much more. Ron didn't overthink or waste a person's time. He was so good at analyzing, understanding, and teaching how to use nuance to improve that his advice was as golden as it was quick.

Actions

1. Inventory your existing capacity.
2. Add complementary skills.
3. Track progress or regress.
4. Practice as much as you can.
5. Expand your experience.
6. Build confidence in layers.
7. Get granular.

HOW I GET BETTER

Peter Lynch, Head of Global Talent, Great-West Financial

I keep getting better by focusing on progress instead of perfection. Perfection is a killer of movement, because it seems too big. When I shrink down what I am trying to attain to something more manageable, I can see the progress I'm making and use that momentum to keep moving forward. One way I accomplish this is by using a "what today?" technique. I don't allow myself to write down any action item or goal without defining what I will do today to accomplish it. This forces me into action, and multiple little actions creates the momentum I need to win and get better.

CHAPTER 12

What Matters

How a Speech About Hunting Knife Safety Changed My Life

Our greatest fear should not be of failure, but of
succeeding at something that doesn't really matter.

—D. L. MOODY

Did you ever wonder how you ended up doing what you do now
for a living? I know how I became a professional speaker, but it
took me twenty-five years to figure out why.

It was all because of a humiliating abject failure on my
part. As a kid, I wasn't very good at much of anything. I was
blessed with great parents, and I was fortunate to grow up on a
working farm, where I developed a strong work ethic (not that
there was a choice).

Being overweight, no good at sports, and an honor student
was a trifecta for getting beat up. Frequently. I didn't have an

unhappy childhood per se, but it was fraught with obstacles and challenges.

At the ripe age of ten, I was a member of 4-H, a terrific youth organization that was formed in 1902 in my home state of Ohio. At the time, it served primarily rural youth, but today it boasts 6 million student members and 25 million alumni. The name of my 4-H club (I'm not making this up) was the Happy Hayseeds.

I can still remember the 4-H Pledge, which could be central to what I've shared in this book:

> *I pledge my head to clearer thinking,*
> *My heart to greater loyalty,*
> *My hands to larger service,*
> *and my health to better living,*
> *for my club, my community, my country, and my world.*[1]

I learned much from 4-H, and the early leadership, social skills, and character development have proven invaluable to me.

Among the many competitions 4-H offers for developing life skills is a speaking contest. Not just any speaking contest, but in my day, a safety speaking contest.

The rules were simple: each contestant had three to five minutes to deliver a speech related to the topic. My club needed a representative. I didn't volunteer, but somebody figured, hey, the fat kid gets good grades; he can do it! That's how I entered my first speaking contest.

Keep in mind, this was nearly fifty years ago, and I can remember it as if it were yesterday.

My speech was on "hunting knife safety" (yes, a very popular topic). There was a lectern set up on a six-foot-long table. To my left was an audience composed of my competitors and their parents. To my right was another six-foot-long table with three judges seated behind it.

Let's pause: Have you ever done so badly, been so humiliated, and failed so completely that the memory is etched in your mind? We all have. My first time was that day.

I could feel the blood rising in my neck. I stumbled, fumbled, started, stuttered, stopped, and tried again. It was the longest several minutes of my young life. Needless to say, I didn't win. I didn't place. I didn't get honorable mention or even a ribbon for participating.

And for the first time I can recall, I faced a decision that everyone eventually faces, usually more than once.

When faced with that kind of setback, defeat, or disappointment, what do you do?

A common response is this: "It doesn't matter anyhow." Been there, done that, got the T-shirt. Next!

The longer I've lived, the more I've come to believe that when someone says it really doesn't matter, more often than not, it really does. But saying it doesn't is a way to minimize the pain and disappointment and to quickly move on.

There is another response to situations like that. That comeback is, "It really matters."

And that is the decision I made. I don't take credit for advanced maturity or wisdom. If I had to name a factor, I would attribute it to my parents, who did their best to raise me right. But as embarrassed as I was, I reached a decision: "This is important. I never want to feel this way again when I speak in public. I want to master this."

And that choice started me on my journey. I entered every public speaking contest for young people I could find. Rotary, Ruritan, Optimist Oratorical: those were just a few of the organizations that offered young people the chance to develop their speaking skills.

I watched and learned and I studied and practiced, all in pursuit of one thing: getting better.

Recently I asked myself, "What would have happened had I done okay?" What would I be doing now if I had finished first or second or third and decided that I'd tried something new and done pretty well, so, what's next? I don't know for sure, but I'm pretty certain I wouldn't be a professional speaker.

There is a belief that those who go on to accomplish great things got their start with a success that whetted their appetite for that endeavor. That may happen sometimes.

But at other times success is born in dismal failure. The kind of negative emotion that you never want to experience again propels you to overcome, to master, to triumph. I don't want to sound melodramatic, but that is my story. And maybe it's your story too. As many of us succeed "despite" as "because of." Becoming good and continuing to get better isn't always or even usually the result of superior genetics or fortuitous circumstance. It is about making a decision—and then doing something about it.

I've learned that leaders—in any arena—know what truly matters. That makes them men and women of principle and conviction. But that isn't enough.

Here's how to know what really matters and make it count to others.

WHAT MATTERS TO YOU?

How do you answer the question of what matters to you? Many things matter a little, but only a few things matter a lot. If everything mattered equally, nothing would matter much. Separating and dicing what's truly significant in your life is necessary unless you want to be whiplashed from one activity to another, never knowing where to focus your primary attention. Those are the things you spend the most time, energy, emotion, and money on. They are the things that get you excited or up in arms or activated.

So, when you are reflecting on the bigger issues of your life, contemplate what matters most in your

- life
- relationships
- business
- faith

MEANING SHOWS YOU WHAT MATTERS

"Man cannot stand a meaningless life."

—CARL JUNG

When you don't see much meaning in what you do, you won't bring much value to what you do.

Showing people the meaning in their work helps make it matter to them. How can you do that?

Meaning in what you do is either inherent or infused.

It is easy to spot the significance in some instances, such as a nonprofit that serves the homeless, or a biotech firm that is on the leading edge of cancer research. In these cases, everyone playing different roles needs to be reminded how what they do supports that greater meaning.

Sometimes the work itself doesn't have readily apparent meaning, so you need to infuse it with reasons that matter. How you do your work, why you do it, and who you do it for are all areas where meaning can be found. Leaders are able to make the important matter to others as well.

I was once asked by someone who couldn't find his singular purpose in life what he should do. I encouraged the person to keep looking for what that purpose might be, but in the interim to do the things he did each day intentionally. My friend was looking for his singular and overarching purpose. I was suggesting he find a micro-purpose or higher reason for the things that he did.

If there isn't a higher meaning—and often there isn't—in what you do each day, then do the work meaningfully. If you can't find the purpose of your life, pursue the purpose within the moment.

COMMITMENT PROVES WHAT YOU THINK MATTERS

"If you have some respect for people as they are, you can be more effective in helping them to become better than they are."

—JOHN W. GARDNER

When you commit to support others in their quest for better, that is the best way to demonstrate that what you feel really matters.

Commitment is the price anyone pays to get remarkable results.

Care and concern for those you lead, work with, or serve are evidence that your efforts at improvement aren't just a self-serving attempt to get ahead at their expense. Rather, they are proof of a belief in doing your best work and continuing to improve and refine it.

Commitment is a decision about what you'll do that is independent of the way you feel. Feelings can be short-lived and fickle, but a commitment indicates that you've carefully counted the cost and will do what you say even when the feelings ebb.

You will learn greatly when you commit to teaching and showing others how to better their best. Encouragement to start the process, or continue it, is valuable, as are the recognition and appreciation of those who do good work.

MAKE YOUR PERFORMANCES MATTER AND MAKE THEM BETTER

"Wherever you find yourself and in whatever circumstances, give an impeccable performance."

—EPICTETUS

Blogger Benjamin Hardy says it eloquently: "The more successful you become, the less you can justify low quality. The more focused you must become. The more consistently your daily behaviors must be high quality—and increasingly higher quality."[2]

I am inspired by performances of great mastery. The most widely viewed of these performances are typically done at athletic events, such as the Olympics, or on professional sports teams, or at events such as concerts and plays. But a great performance by a skilled customer service rep, a repair technician, a middle manager presenting to her team, or a restaurant operator delivering an extraordinary dining experience can be just as inspiring, and maybe more so.

Why? We realize that few of us are going to reach enormous levels of public attention in our performances. But the examples I just cited remind us that the regular things done each day can inspire others, and that we all can do them a little better tomorrow with a commitment to keep getting better.

An impeccable performance at your work, at the shelter you volunteer at on weekends, or while coaching your daughter's soccer team may never reach the attention of more than a few. But it can still be a reminder about the power of doing a thing to the best of one's ability and a commitment to be even better the next time it is done.

NO CONCLUSION

Talking about how you can better your best requires the use of techniques and lists to make the concepts understandable and applicable. But constant improvement isn't linear, a straight superhighway to getting better described in three or six or ten steps. We like to think that things can be that way, but they usually aren't.

There is no conclusion to getting better because none of us knows how good we can be. Our potential principle has no end point. The best single strategy I can offer is to strive to make bettering your best a mind-set first and a habit second. Always be thinking about how you can do a little better the things that are important to you. Find a way every day to enhance, enrich, or improve something you do for yourself and for others.

And remember: knowing what matters and working with like-minded individuals doesn't just make you better. It also betters your

- home
- work
- community
- nation
- world

You need to better your best, and the world needs it too.

Actions

1. Clarify what matters most to you.
2. Make the important things matter to others with meaning and commitment.
3. Teach, encourage, and recognize improvement in others.
4. Make your performances matter.
5. Make a mind-set and a habit better.

Acknowledgments

It takes a team to create a good book, and I'm fortunate to have many great people on my team. I'd like to thank: Matt Yates, at Yates and Yates, my literary agent and great friend who enjoys many of the same finer things in life that I do.

Webb Younce, my excellent editor on this project who truly helped make this a better book, as well as the entire team at Thomas Nelson.

My highly successful friends who shared how they get better: Dr. Nido Qubein, John Bledsoe, Joe Calloway, Larry Winget, Randy Pennington, Scott McKain, Ken Philbrick, Peter Lynch, Marty Grunder, and Mark Shupe.

Peter Lynch and Eric Chester, who were two key brainstorming and sound-boarding partners. They are also two close friends of many years.

Dannielle Thompson, Helen Broder, and Rebecca Huron, who help keep me booked and busy and are an invaluable part of the Sanborn & Associates, Inc., team.

The Five Friends who are, first and foremost, my closest friends and confidants, and second, who are inspiring business partners on several collaborative efforts. They are Joe Calloway,

Scott McKain, Randy Pennington, and Larry Winget (and to avoid confusion, I am the fifth friend).

My boys, Hunter and Jackson, who make me proud to be their father. I live my life in hopes of inspiring them to fully express their potential.

And of course, my beautiful wife, Darla, who is my toughest and best critic when it comes to my speaking and writing. She has been the love of my life for more than twenty years.

Sixteen Combinations of Matrix and Breakthrough Improvement

DISRUPT YOUR THINKING

On a topic with opposing positions, learn enough to argue convincingly for the perspective that is not your own.

Search out beliefs that are either wrong or no longer serve you well.

Use the "blank slate" technique: What would you do in your business or career if you were starting over?

DISRUPT YOUR PERFORMANCE

Pick a process or routine to change, whether it's how you conduct a meeting, how you prepare for a sales call, or how you present to your team. Switch it up by finding one new and different thing to try.

Ask someone you trust to give you unvarnished negative feedback about what you need to change or do differently to improve.

Observe someone who does the same thing you do or something similar. What does he or she do differently than you? What can you learn from that person's approach?

DISRUPT YOUR LEARNING

Read (or reread) a classic book on your primary area of expertise. What has changed in the field since the book was written? What hasn't?

Do a quick dive on a subject that you've never thought about learning anything about before.

What modes of learning (classroom, webinar, independent study, etc.) do you use least? Schedule a learning session using that mode.

DISRUPT YOUR REFLECTION

Select a different spot from your usual one to do some reflection. If you usually do so in a quiet location, go somewhere noisy. Are you able to overcome the situational challenge?

Identify the ruts in your reflection. What makes you resist investing the effort? What do you do during introspection that bores you?

Consider the alternatives—if any—to reflection. Are there other processes that would give you a similar result?

ENGAGE OTHERS IN YOUR THINKING

If you read a book by an author that was really helpful, see what else he or she has written and read more.

Buy a cup of coffee for a friend and interview him or her about the most important things that your friend has learned in his or her life.

Send someone you admire two to three brief questions and ask if he or she would be willing to answer via e-mail.

ENGAGE OTHERS IN YOUR PERFORMANCE

Who do you consider among the best at what you do? Study how they do what they do.

Enlist a coach to help with a single, particular skill you would like to improve.

Consider how to involve others directly in your work to make it more engaging and interactive.

ENGAGE OTHERS IN YOUR LEARNING

Keep two lists of things you learn from engaging others, one for good ideas and practices and one for bad ideas and practices. Learn from both the good and the bad.

Ask your wisest advisers what one book they recommend you read.

Create a private social media group focused on improving a particular process or skill and ask like-minded individuals to share ideas.

ENGAGE OTHERS IN YOUR REFLECTION

Ask a wise friend for his or her best practices of reflection.

Do a reflection session with a spouse or close friend and ask each other stimulating questions for introspection.

Read some of the ancient mystics and religious writers you admire and learn how they cultivated their inner life.

(RE)FOCUS YOUR THINKING

Record the most significant lesson you learn each day.

What topics do you read about that fall into the category of interesting rather than informative? Could you free up time by dropping or replacing them?

Identify trending topics and which will have the most impact on your business. Pick one or two to think about and study now.

(RE)FOCUS YOUR PERFORMANCE

What did you do in the past that you need to start doing again?

Survey your activity for the past two weeks. What three or four behaviors or actions created the best results?

What can you do to eliminate distractions from the important things you do each day?

(RE)FOCUS YOUR LEARNING

Schedule a thirty-minute learning-only session devoid of any distractions or interruptions.

Consider whether what you are currently learning is in alignment with your most important goals and highest priorities.

What do you need to "unlearn"—that is, what did you formerly believe that you no longer believe to be true?

(RE)FOCUS YOUR REFLECTION

Have you used reflection and introspection in the past? If so, are you still doing it? If not, why?

Spend one reflection session on each of the four quadrants in the Potential Matrix (yes, it is possible to reflect on reflection).

Schedule fifteen minutes a day for reflection.

INCREASE YOUR THINKING CAPACITY

Start proactively thinking fifteen minutes each day about your life in general or your profession in particular, with the goal of thirty minutes each day over time.

Research the best blog you can find on thinking better, and read it regularly.

Do a deeper dive on something you've been thinking about— get granular.

INCREASE YOUR PERFORMANCE CAPACITY

What skills-based training would most benefit you? Sign up for a course.

Make time to practice—role-playing, rehearsing, or doing something specific to improve your skills.

Pick some new activity to try, regardless of the outcome, to build the first layer of confidence.

INCREASE YOUR LEARNING CAPACITY

Get better at learning. Study keys to learning faster, retaining more of what you learn, or engaging new modalities of learning.

Think about what new skill you could develop that would most complement your primary skills.

Pick a subject you very much want your son or daughter to understand and teach it to him or her.

INCREASE YOUR REFLECTION CAPACITY

Consider how you could you use reflection and introspection more effectively.

Keep a journal of your reflections.

Periodically make time to reflect during the day. Pick something that is vexing or challenging you and reflect on what you need to think, feel, or do about it.

The Eight Questions for Making Your Best Better

MATRIX IMPROVEMENT:

How can I improve my performance?
How can I improve my learning?
How can I improve my reflection?
How can I improve my thinking?

BREAKTHROUGH IMPROVEMENT:

What or who in my life needs to be disrupted?
How can I engage others better?
Where do I need to (re)focus?
How can I increase my skills and abilities capacity?

Notes

Chapter 1: The Potential Principle

1. *Top Gun*, directed by Tony Scott (1986; Hollywood: Paramount, 2006), DVD.

Chapter 2: Why Get Better?

1. Ben Lowings, "Cannibal Theory for Locust Swarms," BBC News, updated May 12, 2008, http://news.bbc.co.uk/2/hi/7395356.stm.

2. See Shirley Wang, "Surgery's Far Frontier: Head Transplants," *Wall Street Journal*, June 5, 2015, http://www.wsj.com/articles/surgerys-far-frontier-head-transplants-1433525830.

Chapter 4: Escalating Performance

1. "Jack LaLanne, 'Godfather of Fitness,' Dies at 96," *Consumer Reports*, January 24, 2011, http://www.consumerreports.org/cro/news/2011/01/jack-lalanne-godfather-of-fitness-dies-at-96/index.htm.

2. George Leonard, *Mastery: The Keys to Long-Term Success and Fulfillment*, reissue ed. (New York: Plume, 1992), 14–15.

3. Anders Ericsson and Robert Pool, "Malcolm Gladwell Got Us Wrong: Our Research Was Key to the 10,000-Hour Rule, but Here's What Got Oversimplified," *Salon*, April 10, 2016, http://www.salon.com/2016/04/10/malcolm_gladwell_got_us

_wrong_our_research_was_key_to_the_10000_hour_rule_but
_heres_what_got_oversimplified/, emphasis added.

4. Ibid.

5. Atul Gawande, *The Checklist Manifesto: How to Get Things Right* (New York: Metropolitan Books, 2009).

Chapter 5: Leveraged Learning

1. Cristine Andes, "Waiting Tables to NASA: How Education Changed My Life," *Shriver Report*, October 4, 2013, http:// shriverreport.org/waiting-tables-to-nasa-how-education-changed -my-life-cristine-andes/.

2. Kevin Kelly, *The Inevitable: Understanding the 12 Technological Forces That Will Shape Our Future* (New York: Viking, 2016), 10–11.

3. Charlie Munger, commencement address, USC Law School, May 13, 2007, posted at Joe Koster, *Value Investing World* (blog), May 17, 2007, https://aboveaverageodds.files.wordpress .com/2009/12/charlie-munger-usc-law-school-commencement -may-2007.pdf.

4. John Dunlosky et al., "Which Study Strategies Make the Grade?," Association for Psychological Science website, January 10, 2013. Accessed October 25, 2016, http://www.psychological science.org/index.php/news/releases/which-study-strategies -make-the-grade.html.

5. Shane Parrish, "The Best Way to Learn Anything: The Feynman Technique," *Farnam Street* (blog), April 26, 2012, https://www.farnamstreetblog.com/2012/04/learn-anything -faster-with-the-feynman-technique/.

Chapter 6: Deeper Thinking

1. "NGA Sculpture Galleries: Auguste Rodin" (Adobe Flash), National Gallery of Art website, zone 2, accessed October 25, 2016, http://www.nga.gov/collection/sculpture/flash/zone2–2.htm.

2. Adrienne M. Harrison, *A Powerful Mind: The Self-Education of George Washington* (Lincoln, NE: Potomac Books, 2015), 56.

3. Frank Rodriquez, "Learning How to Learn: Reflecting on the Work of Alvin Toffler," *Insight* (the blog of the University of Oklahoma College of Liberal Studies), April 30, 2015, http://clsblog.ou.edu/learning-learn-reflecting-work-alvin-toffler/.

4. Mike Sager, "What I've Learned: Jack Nicholson," *Esquire*, January 29, 2007, http://www.esquire.com/entertainment/interviews/a1956/esq0104-jan-jack/.

Chapter 7: Insightful Introspection

1. Teddy Wayne, "The End of Reflection," Future Tense, *New York Times*, June 11, 2016, http://www.nytimes.com/2016/06/12/fashion/internet-technology-phones-introspection.html.

Chapter 8: Disrupt Yourself

1. Sandi Mann, "Why Are We So Bored?" *Guardian* (UK), April 24, 2016, https://www.theguardian.com/lifeandstyle/2016/apr/24/why-are-we-so-bored.

2. C. S. Lewis, *Surprised by Joy: The Shape of My Early Life* (Orlando: Harcourt, 1966), 206–7.

Chapter 9: (re)Focus

1. Claudia Wallis, "The Multitasking Generation," *Time*, March 19, 2006, http://www.fritzhubbard.org/words/The_Multitasking_Generation.pdf.

2. Nancy K. Napier, "The Myth of Multitasking," *Psychology Today*, May 12, 2014, https://www.psychologytoday.com/blog/creativity-without-borders/201405/the-myth-multitasking.

3. Tonya Basu, "Something Called 'Attention Residue' Is Ruining Your Concentration," *New York: Science of US*, January 21, 2016. http://nymag.com/scienceofus/2016/01/attention-residue-is-ruining-your-concentration.html.

4. Rick Warren, "The Battle for Your Mind," sermon delivered at the Desiring God 2010 National Conference, October 1, 2010, http://www.desiringgod.org/messages/the-battle-for-your-mind.

Chapter 10: Engage Others

1. Uncommon Friends Foundation, *Lessons Learned from the Uncommon Friends: A Curriculum for Emerging Leaders* (Fort Myers, Uncommon Friends Foundation, n.d.), 2, https://uncommonfriends.org/docs/lessons1.pdf.
2. Anders Ericsson, quoted in Cory Turner, "Practice Makes Possible: What We Learn by Studying Amazing Kids," June 1, 2016, from an interview with Ericsson, as heard on *All Things Considered*, NPR, http://www.npr.org/sections/ed/2016/06/01/479335421/practice-makes-possible-what-we-learn-by-studying-amazing-kids.

Chapter 11: Increasing Capacity

1. T. Rees Shapiro, "No Sweat: High School Junior Completes 7,000 Pull-Ups to Shatter World Records," *Washington Post*, May 17, 2016, https://www.washingtonpost.com/news/education/wp/2016/05/17/no-sweat-high-school-junior-completes-7000-pull-ups-to-shatter-world-records/.
2. Cheryl Snapp Conner, "Becoming Indispensable: Zenger Folkman Feature in *Harvard Business Review* Gives New and Proven Strategies for Taking Careers to the Top," Business Wire, September 21, 2011, http://www.businesswire.com/news/home/20110921005181/en/Indispensable-Zenger-Folkman-Feature-Harvard-Business-Review.
3. Geoffrey Colvin, "What It Takes to Be Great," *Fortune*, October 19, 2006, http://archive.fortune.com/magazines/fortune/fortune_archive/2006/10/30/8391794/index.htm.
4. Center for Creative Leadership, https://www.ccl.org.

Chapter 12: What Matters

1. "4-H Pledge," 4-H.org, accessed October 26, 2016, http://4-h.org/about/what-is-4-h/4-h-pledge/
2. Benjamin P. Hardy, "Why Most People Will Never Be Successful," *The Mission*, June 25, 2016, https://medium.com/the-mission/why-most-people-will-never-be-successful-aa52e333a59c#.u47wd4my1.

About the Author

Mark Sanborn is the president of Sanborn & Associates, Inc., an idea lab for leadership development and turning ordinary into extraordinary. Listed by GlobalGurus.org as one of the top thirty leadership experts in the world, Mark is an award-winning speaker and the author of eight books, including *The Fred Factor*, an international bestseller and a *New York Times*, *Business Week*, and *Wall Street Journal* bestseller. He lives in Highlands, Colorado, with his wife and family.

📞 (303) 683-0714

🇪 @Mark_Sanborn

🖥 MarkSanborn.com